WOMAN'S OWN BOOK OF
house plants

WOMAN'S OWN BOOK OF
house plants

William Davidson

HAMLYN
London · New York · Sydney · Toronto

© The Hamlyn Publishing Group Limited 1969
THE HAMLYN PUBLISHING GROUP LTD.
LONDON · NEW YORK · SYDNEY · TORONTO
Hamlyn House, Feltham
Middlesex, England

Second impression, 1971
ISBN 0 600 40350 5
Printed in Czechoslovakia, by PZ Bratislava
52030

Contents

The Editor is grateful to Thomas Rochford and Sons Ltd. for providing us with facilities for photography at their house plant nursery. Thanks also go to Amateur Gardening, J. E. Downward, Mr Peter Hunt, Mr A. J. Huxley, Mr Harry Smith and Miss Violet Stevenson for providing us with colour and black and white photographs. Miss A. E. Burridge of the Kenway Florist, London S.W.5., and Cogswells (Premier Garden Sales) Ltd., kindly provided us with plant containers for photographic purposes. Mr R. Gilbert, Mr and Mrs L. Murray and Mr and Mrs D. Romer were kind enough to allow us to take photographs of house plants in their homes.

Colour Illustrations

between pages

Introduction

The popularity of house plants has now reached such proportions that it is unusual to visit a house in which no plant at all is grown. One can confidently predict that this current enthusiasm will continue for many years, especially as the proportions of modern living rooms with their often rather severe outlines and large windows are particularly well suited to this kind of plant display. Once bitten by the bug of house plant growing, the tendency seems to be to utilise every possible corner of the house – so beware!

This book is designed for those who want to know something about the culture of plants indoors without necessarily delving too deeply into their background and nomenclature. For information I have drawn on over 20 years of experience of growing, exhibiting, talking, advising – in fact, almost 'living' house plants. And, above all, I have kept in mind the endless stream of questions that have been asked over the years.

Though I have not knowingly sought information from the book of any other author, I feel sure that many of my acquaintances will, however, recognise some of my material as their personal opinions. For this I apologise, if apology is necessary.

I am often asked the simple question, 'What actually is a house plant?' The answer is equally simple: 'Any plant that forms a permanent part of room decoration'. So, my Granny, in the far north of Scotland, will be pleased to know that her 'shamrock' (oxalis), humble though it is, can lay claim to being a house plant.

Perhaps I should point out that I have not set out to give brief information on the largest possible number of plants but have endeavoured to discuss fewer plants more fully, and provide more general advice on plant culture indoors. Well-grown house plants, attractively displayed, can add greatly to the pleasures of the home.

W. Davidson

Chapter 1
Selection and Display

Eventual success with house plants depends very often on the quality of plant initially purchased. Average indoor conditions, on the whole, leave much to be desired when seeking the ideal environment in which to grow plants of any kind. Consequently, it stands to reason that a plant of inferior quality, when introduced to room conditions, will quickly deteriorate, whereas the robust plant with a vigorous, healthy root system, and free from pests, will have a better chance of survival.

Doubtless, the High Street florist would take exception if his customers were to go around knocking his plants from their pots to ensure that they were about to purchase a plant with ample strong, clean, roots. There are, however, other ways of detecting good from bad; and one of the most important points is to ensure that plants are actively growing, and not stunted or limp at the tips. Even in winter, greenhouse-grown pot plants should make a reasonable amount of growth, though there are a few exceptions, such as the Rubber Plant (*Ficus elastica decora*), which is described on p. 44.

If a plant has a fresh, crisp appearance this is another point in favour of purchase. Staked plants should look as if the growth is actually climbing the stake, and one ought to avoid plants that are hanging limply around their support. Hard-baked or thoroughly saturated composts are both signs of mismanagement on the part of the supplier, and are two more reasons for directing your purse and your footsteps to the next shop along the road.

WELL-FURNISHED PLANTS

The professional grower is always impressed on seeing what he terms 'a well-furnished plant'. By this he means a plant of full appearance with leaves all the way down the stem; and, given the choice, he would invariably select the smaller, well-furnished plant in preference to the tall, leggy one. Production of such a plant takes more time and requires frequent pinching of leading shoots to encourage a bushy appearance, particularly so in respect of ivies, so one should expect to pay a little more for it. Missing, yellow, or damaged leaves are further indications of indifferent culture and handling.

DEFECTS TO LOOK FOR IN FLOWERING PLANTS

With flowering pot plants it is also important to look for the same defects that one might expect to find in foliage plants: yellow and missing leaves, an untidy appearance and so on. Equally, or perhaps more important, is the need to buy plants that are not 'blown' or in full flower, though it is also important that flowering plants should not be too backward when purchased. The aim should be to select plants with a

9

reasonable amount of colour showing and plenty of young buds still to open that will give you pleasure in the months to come. There are exceptions, though; the pleasure of seeing a friend's face light up on being presented with something as exciting as an *Azalea indica* in full bloom can make the lasting qualities of the plant seem unimportant.

PLASTIC POTS

Much controversy still reigns over the pros and cons of plastic pots compared to clay ones. A few years ago I would have unhesitatingly selected the plant growing in a clay pot in preference to an equally good, often better plant growing in a plastic pot. Neither does it seem so long ago that the rather conservative race of

people generally referred to as gardeners, or growers, were shaking their heads disapprovingly as they uttered, 'You'll never grow a hydrangea in a plastic pot'. The same was said about producing cyclamen in plastic pots, and subsequently the same heads were shaking at the thought of growing poinsettias in such containers. However, as we all know, these plants are now almost all grown in the lighter pot, and it would seem that the clay pot with its many drawbacks is dying a comparatively rapid death. Have no qualms about selecting the plastic pot; most plants do equally well in them and many do very much better.

A slight change in growing technique is necessary for plants in plastic pots, in that they require very much less water than similar plants growing in clay pots.

Some years ago a meticulously controlled experiment was carried out with clay and plastic pots in order to estimate the growth difference of plants grown in identical conditions. It was found that the different pots had very little effect on the plants. Where a mixed batch of pots was watered according to the requirements of the clay pots, the plastic ones became much too wet, and when the treatment was reversed, the compost in the clay pots became much too dry. In every other respect the clean, light and easily handled plastic pot gave a very good account of itself.

When growing saintpaulias, the plastic pot has a marked advantage over the clay, as the latter absorbs moisture that will quickly rot through any leafstalks that may rest on the rim of the pot. An aluminium foil,

A well-lit room kept at an even temperature provides ideal conditions for most house plants. This room extension is made much more attractive by such decoration

Opposite page: **Clockwise from left,** *Calathea louisae, Aralia elegantissima, Dracaena godseffiana* **Florida Beauty and** *Maranta leuconeura kerchoveana*

The trailing stems of *Ficus pumila* provide a striking contrast to the bold, variegated leaves of *Aglaonema pseudo-bracteatum*

or silver paper protective cover, kneaded around the edge of the clay pot is essential in order to prevent leafstalks becoming wet.

GETTING YOUR PLANTS HOME, UNHARMED

Purchasing a suitable plant is one thing, but taking it from the shop to the home unprotected can often undo all the good work of the nurseryman. So, when acquiring plants during the colder months, adequate wrapping should be insisted on. When making your choice, do not pass too lightly over the clean plant that has been carefully wrapped. Plants, as a rule, leave warm greenhouses and, though they quickly adapt themselves to cooler indoor conditions, a short spell in

below freezing conditions will often prove fatal. The damage may not be apparent until some time later.

Mention of cold conditions suggests a further precaution when making one's purchase. Generally speaking, there are few shops where space is not a permanent problem, and this is frequently made obvious by the number of plants stood outside on the pavement. This may be all very well for the hardier type of indoor plant during the summer months, but the sight of a *Begonia rex* propped against the outside wall of a shop in the middle of March is enough to chill the blood. Need one be warned not to buy from the box outside, or from the inconsiderate person who placed it there?

HOW DIFFICULT IS IT TO GROW?

Of the various house plants available, the majority are comparatively easy to manage and with reasonable care will give several years pleasure, while others are more trying and will test the skill of the most competent house plant grower. Several nurserymen are wise enough to attach labels to their products with clearly printed advice regarding each particular plant, and whether they are easy or difficult to manage indoors. When purchasing plants needing higher temperatures, like codiaeums (crotons) and dieffenbachias, it should be realized that these are expendable and will in some cases give only a few months pleasure, though keen plantsmen seem to manage many of them very well once the plants have settled down in their new environments. But it should not be forgotten that when compared with the often expensive bunch of flowers, the exotic foliage plant is indeed good value for money.

PLANT CONTAINERS AND PLANT DISPLAY

Suitable containers of adequate size are one of the most important aids to plant display, be it a piece of ornamental pottery for a single pot, or an elaborate container for a group of plants. When purchasing an outer decorative pot for a plant already in your possession take the simple precaution of either measuring the plant's pot before setting out on your errand, or, better still, take an empty pot with you of similar size to the one in which your plant is growing. Where possible, containers should be slightly larger than the pot in order that a layer of moist pebbles can be placed in the bottom of the decorative pot for your plant to stand on.

When selecting or making display containers, keep in mind the thought that the height of plants is almost invariably governed by the dimensions of the pot in which the plant is growing. The following approximate guide to relative sizes may be helpful: a $3\frac{1}{2}$-in. diameter pot for a plant about 15in. to 18in. tall; a 5-in. pot for a plant about 20in. to 26in. tall; a 7-in. pot for a plant about $3\frac{1}{2}$ft. to $4\frac{1}{2}$ft. tall; and a 9-in. pot for a plant about 5ft. to 7ft. tall. Plants in larger pots should always be seen before finalising purchase; otherwise, you may, for example, purchase a 4ft. tall monstera plant only to find that the spread of the plant is much too large for the position earmarked for it.

The use of larger containers accommodating a number of plants poses the question of whether one should employ the free-planting method, or simply plunge plant pots to their rims in moist peat. If the first method is adopted the container should be almost filled with compost and the plants placed on the compost in suitable positions, so simplifying the actual planting operation which follows. I would suggest leaving one or two spaces for flowering plants; do this by inserting an empty pot or two which can be easily removed and replaced with a flowering plant at almost any time. When the plants are freely planted, growth will be much more vigorous, but there will be less opportunity for rearranging the plants.

If plants are left in their pots, probably the best plunging medium is moist peat, as plants are easily arranged in this and can be tilted at just the right angle for the finished effect. If the dark peat is found to be objectionable, a scattering of gravel on the surface of the peat will improve appearances. Where plants with differing water requirements are free-planted in the same container it will be wise to strike a happy medium when watering, and, if anything, one should err on the side of dryness rather than making the soil over-moist.

Working with plants one should not be afraid of getting one's hands dirty occasionally, even if it is only to prod a finger into the soil to test its water requirements. Nevertheless, it would be regrettable if the would-be house plant owner were to be put off by my references to soil, peat and the like. Take heart, there

An attractive group – *Begonia rex* (bottom), *Codiaeum reidii* (left), *Kentia belmoreana* (top)

are many other ways of displaying plants, and inspection of the wide variety of plant stands and containers available in almost any good department store or florist's shop will provide ample opportunity for experiment. If space is limited, the standard type of plant trough can be used to get the maximum number of plants into the minimum amount of space. The well-arranged plant table always appeals to me as providing a clean and effective display that is easily maintained.

How much have we to learn about plant display in the living room of around 20ft. by 10ft.? My feeling is that we have a great deal to learn from those living in Continental countries in this respect.

Taking a block of flats (where indoor plants mean so much to those without gardens) on almost any housing estate in this country as a yardstick, I am afraid that the way house plants are displayed compares most unfavourably with similar homes on the other side of the North Sea. Recently I had the pleasure of spending a holiday in Amstelveen, a suburb of Amsterdam, where I lived in a box-shaped room, with a large plate glass window, in a box-shaped block of flats. During the day these flats had little to commend them, other than immaculate council-tended gardens, compared to similar developments here. However, during darkness, when the room lights were switched on, the place became a fascinating fairyland for me. My wife and I walked around and unashamedly stared into many of the delightful rooms with their diffused lights and remarkable range of superbly grown house plants. I got the feeling that our Dutch hosts derived a certain amount of pleasure when someone stopped and paid them the compliment of admiring their contribution to the general charm of the neighbourhood. Need one add that a tour of a similar area here would be a pretty dismal business – and it

The key plant in this arrangement is the handsome cut-leaved *Monstera deliciosa borsigiana*. Its associates (clockwise) are *Dracaena sanderiana*, *Impatiens petersiana*, *Scindapsus aureus* Marble Queen and *Begonia rex*

could all so easily be changed, with a little effort.

INGREDIENTS FOR SUCCESS

Doubtless the bare minimum of curtain draped around the windows of Dutch homes during the day is one reason for them being able to grow plants of infinitely better quality than most of us here. I include myself, as I have been fighting a losing battle with my wife over the years to have windows freed from light obstruction. Alas, privacy is still more important. Of all the considerations when arranging plants indoors, perhaps the most important is to ensure that they have a light position in which to grow.

A further possible reason for our Continental neighbours' success with plants is that they always seem to have plenty; seldom less than twenty in the average living room. There seems little doubt that plants do better when grouped together, be they in the greenhouse or the home, and the single plant with a room to itself rarely prospers. Like ourselves, plants seem to approve of company, and soon deteriorate in solitary confinement.

The Continental grower is more fortunate than his British counterpart in that he has created many more occasions, other than the usual ones, for the giving of flowers and plants as gifts. Birthday and Christmas present-giving times are important, but it is also quite common for the Continental housewife to find a welcoming array of plants and flowers awaiting her on return from her annual summer holiday. Plants play such an important part in room decoration that it is not uncommon to find specially designed plant windows in many homes; these are positioned where plants will not be exposed to strong midday sun. Such windows have deeper than usual tiled sills, and are often provided with suitable drainage, so that there is no concern when water is spilt.

An extension of this idea is the plant room, where the bare minimum of furniture is used and plants are given pride of place. These rooms are not unlike the Victorian conservatory, except for the fact that they are integral parts of the house with large plate glass windows, carpeted floors, and similar comforts.

ARTIFICIAL LIGHTING

When arranging groups of plants or individual plants indoors, particular care must be taken that the lighting is adequate. A plant stood in a dark corner contributes little to the appearance of the room, yet the same plant, artificially lit, improves out of all recognition. Use light to enhance the appearance of your plants in the same way as the shopkeeper does to brighten his wares; though with plants, softer lighting is more effective.

A FIREPLACE DISPLAY

During the summer months the disused fireplace is a favourite position for indoor plants. When such a position is chosen for plants, take the precaution of blocking off the chimney vent with a piece of cardboard, otherwise they will quickly succumb to the draughty conditions. Unless the room is particularly well lit it is better to confine one's choice to the hardier varieties when decorating the fireplace, and preferably to the green-leaved sorts. The fireplace is often the ideal place for arranging a temporary display of plants for a special occasion, when other space may be at a premium.

PARTIES AND HOUSE PLANTS DON'T AGREE

Here I might well add a further note of warning; at party time plants will be much safer if they are transferred to an upstairs bedroom. Guests who are having just one more drink pressed on them are not above emptying the unwanted alcohol into the convenient receptacle provided by a plant pot! The damage does not become apparent until some time later, and the plants sudden failure usually remains a mystery.

AUTOMATIC WATERING

In recent years the principle of watering plants by means of capillary attraction has gained many devotees, and much work has been done towards perfecting this method of watering, whereby the plants are stood on a permanently moist base and take up water according to their needs. It is particularly useful if one leads a busy life and cannot attend to the water requirements of plants as often as one should. Equally, it is a boon in the conservatory or greenhouse that is left unattended for most of the day while one is out at work. Capillary watering also presents a method of ensuring that plants have ample moisture at their roots while owners are on holiday. This is particularly useful, as house plants always present a problem at holiday time.

Many plastics' manufacturers have developed trays that need little more than a supply of water from a 'header' tank, or bottle, and a 2-in. layer of sharp sand in the tray to become almost fool-proof capillary units. The water level in the reservoir tank should be topped up periodically; after initial experiments it becomes a simple matter to adjust the apparatus to ensure that the sand is maintained at the ideal degree of moistness for the plants' needs.

A make-shift capillary unit can be made simply by filling a shallow baking tin with sand and keeping it moist by means of a watering-can. The sand, for best results, should be kept quite wet, but avoid getting the sand into a puddled condition as, in this case, the plants would suffer from waterlogging and would quickly deteriorate.

Thin-based plastic pots are ideal for capillary watering, as the compost in the pot and the wet sand come into direct contact, thus ensuring that water is drawn up from the sand immediately. Holes in the bottom of clay pots should be plugged with a piece of fibre-glass padding which will act as a wick, so bridging the gap between compost and sand. The plant pots must be gently pushed into the sand when placing them in position, and it is important that the soil in the pot should be watered before placing it on the sand so that capillary attraction will commence. Further watering should not be necessary.

Chapter 2
Routine Culture

Times out of number I have been asked for advice on the most suitable plant for a dark corner. My reaction is to suggest the dear old Cast Iron Plant (aspidistra) which will tolerate the most trying conditions without batting an eyelid, or, should we say, shedding a leaf. However this advice is not always met with approval, so, if you have a dark corner and the aspidistra is not acceptable, the only solution is to see your electrician and have a light fitted there. Years of experience have shown that a light, airy room provides by far the most suitable conditions for the majority of indoor plants offered for sale today. Oddly enough, though, many of them will also do very well in artificially lit rooms. There is, however, one important precaution; though adequate light is of the utmost importance, care must be taken to ensure that some protection is provided against strong, direct sunlight.

THE IMPORTANCE OF FEEDING

Beginners with house plants launch out with every good intention, purchasing the best plants, suitable containers, and so on, yet, after a month or two, the plants have much smaller new leaves than they should have, lose their lower ones, and take on a generally hard appearance. Why? In the majority of cases, it is because feeding is being neglected.

The efficient nurseryman sends out established plants, be they in the smallest 'tots' or the larger 10in. size pot. From the time they have become established in their pots, large or small, the plants will have received regular feeding with a balanced fertiliser. Should this supply of nutrient suddenly stop when the plant leaves the nursery, a gradual process of deterioration will take place; hence, smaller and harder leaves.

For the sake of convenience most nurserymen use easily applied liquid fertilisers, though the wise ones occasionally ring the changes and give applications of powdered fertiliser during the growing season.

SIMPLE RULES

There are a few simple rules to follow when feeding house plants. One should ensure that the compost in the pot is moist before applying fertilisers, as dry roots are very easily damaged, particularly so if one is misguided enough to use plant food in excess of recommended requirements. Always follow the manufacturers' directions for they have carefully experimented in order to arrive at the correct strength and rate of use for their products. Some plants do benefit from additional

A gay container can often enhance the charms of house plants. Shown here, left to right, are a tradescantia, *Grevillea robusta* (back), *Peperomia sandersii* and a hedera

16

Opposite: A cool, light room provides ideal conditions for colourful cyclamen, here displayed with *Begonia rex* (in foreground)

A group planting of *Ficus elastica tricolor* (left), *Ficus benjamina* (right), and the poinsettia, Paul Mikkelsen (foreground)

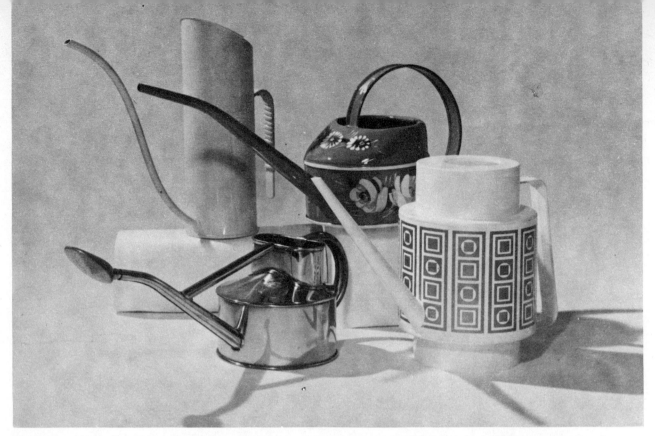

Watering, in the last resort, can be done with any jug or container but it is infinitely easier and more pleasant with watering-cans such as those shown above in metal or plastic (bottom right)

feeding, and advice on this matter is given under the descriptions of individual plants.

WINTER TREATMENT

On the whole, winter feeding is an unnecessary extravagance, but if a plant produces new leaves in winter it will need a fertiliser that has a low nitrogen content to encourage the production of firm rather than soft leaves. The composition of fertilisers should be clearly marked on the container, and your sundries-man or florist will be able to advise you on the most suitable one to use.

WATERING

The failure of almost 75 per cent. of all the plants that eventually find their way to the dustbin can be traced to the over-indulgent housewife who is ever ready with the watering can. Strangely enough, it is misguided kindness on the part of the householder to feel that the plant needs a little something almost every time he or she has a cup of coffee. Much of the damage can also be attributed to the oft-repeated advice, 'Drop it in a bucket of water, wait until all the bubbles stop coming up and your plant will be sufficiently moist'. To my mind, 'sufficiently waterlogged' would be a better interpretation of the plant's condition.

This treatment may be all very well for the dry azalea, hydrangea, or even the house plant of the aphelandra type which has been allowed to become very dry, but for the majority of plants it is not advisable. In the greenhouse, however, where moisture in any shape or form is a blessing on a hot day, plunging pots in a bucket of water can have its advantages.

As I travel around the various horticultural shows meeting the gardening – or house-plant-growing – public, I am increasingly aware of the need for some sound advice on the subject of watering. Intelligent questioners say they have purchased a particular plant and would appreciate being told exactly how often it will require watering, and I get the impression that an exact answer of 10.15 a.m. on Tuesday and 3 p.m. on Friday would be quite acceptable. But such a reply would, of course, be ludicrous. Plants are very much like human beings, and, as with humans, no two identical plants reared in similar conditions would require exactly the same treatment in respect of food and liquid nourishment.

So what is the answer? First, there is little doubt that it is best to err on the side of dry conditions rather than wet, and, with the average house plant, to allow the compost to dry out a little between waterings. Bear in mind that roots in a permanent wet compost become lazy and inactive, there being no need for them to forage in search of moisture. An active root system is the perfect anchor for a well-furnished plant, and healthy roots are much more capable of withstanding the indifferent treatment that many indoor plants are often subjected to.

HOW TO TELL WHEN PLANTS NEED WATER?

Often, one is advised to tap the pots with a tool made by fixing a cotton reel on the end of a 2-ft. cane to test the

18

plants' water requirements. A dry pot will give a resonant ring and a wet pot a dull thud. This piece of advice, handed down through gardening books, may apply where the experienced gardener is concerned, but the mind boggles at the thought of the average owner of a few indoor plants performing this percussion exercise, and trying to decide whether it should be one or two egg-cupfuls of water.

Better by far to give plants a good watering by filling the space between the rim of the pot and the compost each time the soil takes on a dry, grey-brown appearance. (Do this twice, allowing the first lot to soak in, if the soil is very dry.) Err on the side of dryness by all means, but guard against excessively dry soil; the mixture must never be so dry that the compost is coming away from the side of the pot. Should this happen, subsequent watering will result in water too rapidly finding its way between soil and pot, thereby preventing the root ball from becoming moistened, and this, after all, is the prime object of watering.

A sluggish soil that drains slowly, or not at all, quickly becomes sour. Remedy this by removing the root ball from the pot in order to unblock the drainage holes; it may be necessary to place a few pieces of broken flower pot (crocks) over the drainage holes of clay pots. Plastic pots are amply provided with drainage holes, and only the presence of worms in the soil would cause the drainage holes to become obstructed.

The majority of house plants seem to enjoy the company of each other, and grow better when they are grouped together. However, the large plant that is well-established will happily endure solitude in its individual corner. Wall brackets, in my opinion, are not suitable for the majority of house plants, except for the real toughies, such as ivies, tradescantias, *Philodendron*

scandens and *Rhoicissus rhomboidea.* Less hardy plants should be placed where their needs can be more readily administered to, and, unless of trailing habit, the majority of smaller plants are really seen to best effect when one looks down on them.

Plants grouped together on a plant table, or in a plant trough, provide a pleasing focal point in the room, besides affording the plants more agreeable conditions in which to grow. Where possible, plants ought to stand on, or be plunged in, a moisture-retaining material of some kind. Sphagnum moss, moist peat, or even wet newspaper can be used for this purpose. So that watering needs can be attended to, care must be taken to ensure that the pots are plunged only to their rims and no further. Moist pebbles, or one of the light-weight aggregates such as Lytag, provide an ideal base for standing pots on. Though pebbles must be kept wet to give a moist atmosphere around plants, it will be detrimental if the plant pot is actually allowed to stand in water.

WHEN TO RE-POT

One other aspect of house plant culture that may be taken as routine is the need to transfer plants to larger containers when the soil becomes exhausted. The appearance of a few wispy roots through the bottom of the pot does not necessarily indicate that the plant is in need of fresh soil. The actual root ball must be inspected by removing the plant from its pot, and if the roots are well matted you may then consider that potting on is necessary.

An emphatic plea – plants should not be knocked out of their pots any more than is absolutely necessary. A friend describes it as resembling a surgical operation from which the plant requires time to recover.

Plastic pots, which have holes all round the perimeter of the base, do not need crocking as an aid to drainage. Clay pots with their single, central drainage hole need this assistance

A TECHNIQUE FOR BEGINNERS

For the experienced gardener potting is a simple enough task, but the average householder invariably approaches it with some misgiving. The novice might benefit by adopting the following method; instead of potting the actual plant, take a pot of the same size as that in which your plant is growing and use it to form a mould in the slightly larger container. It is then a simple task to remove the plant from its pot and drop it into the perfectly shaped hole, having first removed the empty pot.

A SUITABLE COMPOST

The potting on operation is best performed in March or April when roots are active and will quickly get on the move in the new compost. The mixture itself is not so critical as we are sometimes led to believe. Experience has shown that almost all house plants prefer a light, open soil of a spongy texture. To arrive at this, without suggesting ingredients that are often difficult to acquire, use a mix consisting of two-thirds John Innes No. 2 Potting Compost (or No. 3 for larger pots) and one-third clean peat. Naturally enough, some plants will need a different mixture; these will be dealt with in the notes on individual plants.

Premature potting on of house plants is not to be recommended. A good guide is to remove the plants from their pots and to pot on if the roots are well matted, as in the case of the chlorophytum and impatiens shown here

A simple method of potting on. *Opposite page, top:* A pot of the size in which the plant is at present growing is placed inside one of the new size. Compost is then added. *Above:* The inner pot is removed to leave a space equal to the size of the plant's root ball

Below left and right: The plant is placed in the cavity and is made firm in the new compost with the fingers. This method ensures that the root ball is in complete contact with the new compost leaving no air pockets. Over-deep planting is also avoided

Chapter 3
Types of Container

The makers of fancy pots, troughs and such like have not been slow in keeping abreast of the general increase of interest in house plants in recent years. A wide range of designs and materials are available for this purpose and some of these are illustrated on p. 25.

When selecting containers the appearance is, of course, important, but it is also essential to ensure that they are of adequate size and that they are watertight. To obviate the possibility of water seepage damaging furniture, one should take the precaution of placing a cork mat under the container until it is obvious that dampness is not likely to be a problem.

WOODEN CONTAINERS

In spite of all the new materials, plant troughs and boxes made from good quality timber still hold their own and blend perfectly with almost any kind of foliage. Such boxes can be made watertight by inserting a

A pedestal arrangement in which the eye-catching dracaena and begonia are complement-ed by graceful ivies and *Philodendron scandens*

metal liner, or, more cheaply and simply, by using drawing pins to tack a double thickness of polythene to the inside of the box. When using any form of wood preservative for treating boxes prior to planting, care must be taken to ensure that the material is not harmful to plant life.

In most cases it will be advisable to fit legs to the container, or to place it on a table where plants may benefit from the maximum light available. (Only larger plants should actually be placed on the floor.) The fitting of Easy-Glide castors also enables one to move plant boxes back into the warmth of the room in the evening where the plants will be much more comfortable than they would be if left in the cooler window position.

DISH-TYPE CONTAINERS

I find that dish-type containers of fairly generous proportions (deep enough to accommodate a 5-in. pot) are excellent for temporary plant arrangements. The owner of a dozen or so plants will derive much pleasure from displaying them in a group as a change from lining the window-sill or decorating the wall. If the container is first filled with peat, newspaper, or sphagnum moss, which is kept moist, this will ensure that plants remain firmly in position when inserted.

The spikes of distinctive white flowers are the attraction of *Peperomia rotundifolia* shown here with *Chlorophytum capense variegatum* and *Begonia rex*

Opposite: Monstera deliciosa borsigiana (background) and *Philodendron bipinnatifidum* (left), with their fresh green leaves and interesting shape and habit are especially well suited to modern room settings. *Dracaena deremensis* (right) and various hederas are also shown

One precaution is necessary – do not allow the plants to be too congested. There must be sufficient space between each for them to be individually appreciated. Displays of this kind can be dismantled and rearranged weekly and will permit the use of flowering pot plants when they are in season, thus providing an extra touch of colour.

OTHER SUGGESTIONS

The greengrocer's fruit basket is probably the cheapest type of plant container for a group of plants, as it is often available simply for the asking. A sheet of polythene spread over the inside of the basket will be a cheap and effective form of waterproofing; take the precaution of extracting any nails that may be protruding before placing the polythene in position. Copper soup tureens and old brass coal scuttles, if they can be acquired, are also excellent for setting off groups of indoor plants.

SELF-WATERING POTS AND TROUGHS

House plant owners who are obliged to leave their plants unattended for any length of time may well gain from purchasing one of the variety of self-watering pots and troughs that are on the market. Not all of these give the desired results, but the majority, having overcome their teething troubles, are now thoroughly reliable. With these devices, watering is simplified to the point where one merely tops up the water supply at intervals to a clearly marked level. Such containers are also ideal for the plant grower who is at a loss to know what to do with indoor plants when going on vacation. Recently I heard about a *Ficus elastica decora* that grew, in a self-watering pot, from a height of 2ft. to 9ft. in the space of three years. This remarkable rate of growth was, it seems, achieved with the minimum amount of attention.

WALL BRACKETS

One sometimes sees photographs of fashion models in luxurious room settings, in which house plants are displayed to apparent perfection. On seeing the latter, the average reader may be tempted to set forth and purchase an exotically-coloured codiaeum (croton) for placing in a wall bracket where it will blend perfectly with the general décor. Take my advice and refrain from putting anything other than the most durable pot plants in containers attached to a wall. The hot, dry atmosphere that plants will have to contend with when pinned to the wall will, in most instances, result in quite rapid deterioration.

If neglected for only a short time the leaves of the wall plant will quickly take on a dry, almost toasted appearance. When positioning wall brackets it is particularly important to ensure that they are not directly over room heaters; the hot dry air from these would lessen the plant's chance of survival. Also, tiny pots dry out very rapidly, so ensure that brackets are bought which will accommodate a pot of at least $3\frac{1}{2}$in. in diameter so that the plants in them can be thoroughly watered.

Opposite above: The aptly named Shrimp Plant (*Beloperone guttata*) with its showy bracts is an interesting plant for a light position

Left: Tall house plants like *Ficus benjamina* pleasingly accentuate the vertical and horizontal lines of the room and cupboard fittings. This impression is heightened by the repetition provided by the sword-like sansevieria (right foreground)

Variegated plants have especially fine decorative qualities. Centred round the striking, speckled dieffenbachia are, from the left foreground clockwise, *Maranta leuconeura kerchoveana*, codiaeum (croton), *Hedera canariensis, Ficus schrijvereana, Sansevieria trifasciata laurentii, Begonia masoniana, Aphelandra* Silver Beauty and *Peperomia magnoliaefolia*

By extending the window-sill it is possible to convert a living room into a miniature greenhouse. This gay mid-winter picture includes the popular poinsettia, ivies, *Episcia cupreata* in the hanging basket together with a well-flowered *Azalea indica* on the table

HANGING BASKETS

Many of the easier house plants will benefit from a short 'holiday' in the garden during the summer months. In this connection the hanging basket is ideal in that it can be planted and put in position outside in the garden or on the balcony and can be quickly moved to a sheltered spot should the weather become inclement. Although one must agree that the conventional moss-lined basket is probably best, excellent results can be had by lining the basket with black polythene prior to filling with compost and planting. Drainage is essential, so use a skewer to perforate the polythene after planting. Where drips may be a problem there are baskets available with built-in trays.

Right: The house plant enthusiast no longer has to make do with dull containers. These are now available in a wide range of shapes and colours in such materials as clay, pottery, glass and polystyrene. Bamboo-handled miniature tools, also shown here, are useful as well as decorative

For raised, multiple-plant displays, many elegant troughs are obtainable in wood and metal. Wooden and plastic pot covers, as shown in the foreground, can be used to mask ordinary flower pots

Chapter 4
Easily Grown House Plants

Over the years the majority of the plants referred to in this chapter have proved themselves in all manner of conditions, and almost all are on the nurseryman's availability list. Purchase of some will, however, necessitate a special order to your supplier, and the possibility of having to wait until a batch of plants becomes available.

Growing conditions and cultural directions for plants in this group can be generalised, and where special treatment is required this is stated in my notes on individual plants. On the whole, a light position and a temperature in the region of 60°F. (16°C.) is advised. Information on general care (watering, feeding and such like) will be found in Chapter 2, on Routine Culture.

To make reference easy, the plants in this section have been grouped together in their families. There is also a comprehensive index at the end of the book.

THE AROID FAMILY

Plants belonging to the family *Araceae* are frequently referred to as aroids, and they are to be found almost everywhere in the world in one form or another. The Arum Lily is one of the best known members of this botanical grouping.

If our house plant growers were to be deprived of the benefits of any particular family of plants, for some reason or other, one feels that the aroids would be their greatest loss. From this family we get easy plants, difficult ones, flowering plants, and many of the bolder ones so much relied upon for display and general decoration. Almost all of the pot-grown members prefer a temperature in excess of 60°F. (16°C.) and the atmosphere is rarely too humid for them. Yet, one recalls the disastrous cold winter of 1962-63 when many plants were obliged to suffer lower temperatures than were previously thought possible. Although many succumbed, a surprising number pulled through. We learned that when low temperatures were unavoidable the plants tolerated the conditions much more satisfactorily when the soil in the pot was kept almost bone dry. One batch of *Philodendron bipinnatifidum* that we were growing, when treated in this way, survived temperatures that were on many nights down to 34°F. (1°C.).

Monstera deliciosa borsigiana

Really mature plants of monstera would in some cases be large enough to fill the smaller living room, leaving very little space for inhabitants or furniture. Have no fear, though; when confined to smaller pots indoors, the leaves remain of manageable size.

Monstera deliciosa borsigiana, **an easily grown plant with outstanding 'architectural' qualities**

Philodendrons such as the variety Burgundy shown here, make good plants for individual displays against a plain wall of light colouring. Note the mossed stake which aids the growth of this plant and of that shown opposite

Often I am asked what one should do with the freely produced aerial roots of this plant. The answer is to wind them around on top of the soil in the pot, and use string to tie them in position. Make a hole in the compost with a pencil and direct the tip of the root into it; this will keep the young roots under control.

One must be patient in order to appreciate the reason for the name *deliciosa*, as there is nothing about the plant itself to suggest the reason for it. Mature plants of monstera will, in time, produce exquisite, creamy-white inflorescences (very short lived), which eventually develop into fruits of the most unappetising appearance. To sample the fruit at its best one must be patient and leave it on the plant until the outer protective covering begins to disintegrate. Even then it is possible to eat only a little of the fruit, with its elusive pineapple-banana flavour. In Australia it is called the Fruit Salad Plant. I find that it is best to stand the fruit in a jug and to eat a little with a spoon each day as the outer green covering goes through the natural process of peeling itself away from the pulp-like fruit underneath. Do not let the appearance of the edible part put you off – your courage will be well rewarded.

Monstera leaves can be cleaned in the same way as those of other glossy-leaved plants, though great care must be taken not to handle young leaves, which are very easily damaged.

Philodendron bipinnatifidum

This plant is best suited to the more spacious room where its large leaves will have an opportunity to extend to their full spread. Though sometimes offered for sale, smaller plants are not very satisfactory, as the leaves do not show their true character until the plants are growing freely in pots of at least 7 in. in diameter.

Surprisingly enough, I once saw this plant being used as a hanging basket subject in one of the reception areas of a Continental airport. It is comparatively easy to grow so maintenance was little bother, and the plant effectively relieved the emptiness of the high ceiling.

There are several similar philodendrons with leaves radiating from a central crown on petioles 2ft. or more in length. These will develop aerial roots in time, and, as an alternative to tying them together on top of the pot, the roots can be directed into a container of water and allowed to take in moisture from this source. It is also a way of interesting young children in plants for they will be intrigued to see the root action. When a plant is treated in this way it will be found that the compost in the pot requires comparatively little water.

Philodendron Burgundy and P. hastatum

These two plants are both typical of the Aroid Family in their cultural needs. Both benefit if their supporting stakes are clad with a 1- or 2-in. layer of fresh sphagnum moss. If the moss is kept moist, the freely produced aerial roots will quickly find their way into it, and the plant will grow much better as a result. Keeping mossed stakes moist indoors does, however, present a problem. This may be overcome by standing the plant in the bath, or outdoors (on a fine day), and thoroughly soaking the moss with a hand spray. Many of the other aroids will also benefit from the use of similar mossed stakes. These stakes are easily prepared by binding the moss to the stake with plastic-covered wire of neutral colour; plastic wire is preferable as it is non-corrosive.

Philodendron scandens

By far the best known of the philodendrons is *P. scandens*, mainly because of its ability to withstand ill-treatment. It would be nice to say it remains un-scathed, but low temperatures and mishandling soon give the leaves a dry, paper-like appearance instead of their natural glossy green. The American common name, Bathroom Plant, gives a clue to the conditions it likes – a hot and steamy atmosphere. Bathrooms with

Philodendron hastatum, with its distinctive leaves, is a natural choice where sufficient room space is available

a minimum temperature of 60°F. (16°C.) are ideal, and it would be unwise to subject *P. scandens* (The Sweet-heart Plant, as it is called in this country) to the tempera-ture fluctuations of the average bathroom, which is an icebox for most of the day. Fluctuating temperatures are more damaging to plants than those that are constant, even though slightly below the recom-mended level.

THE ARALIA FAMILY

Plants belonging to the *Araliaceae*, the Aralia Family, are native to both tropical and temperate parts of the world and include many with ornamental foliage and attractive habit.

Fatsia japonica and Fatshedera lizei variegata

When considering this family we are immediately faced with a plant that masquerades under two names – *Fatsia japonica*, and *Aralia sieboldii*. In common with the ivies, which also belong to this family, the aralias are dual-purpose plants in that they may be planted

Opposite: Fatshedera lizei variegata – an excellent choice for the back row of a group of plants or for display as a single specimen

Fatsia japonica variegata: in this variegated form slightly more difficult to grow than the ordinary species, but more imposing

out in a sheltered spot in the garden when they have outgrown their allotted space indoors, or, as so often happens, they are planted out as an alternative to throwing them in the dustbin. The green form of *Fatsia japonica* is an 'easy doer' that will, with proper attention, make a substantial plant, though this will take some time in room conditions.

In common with almost all variegated plants, *F. japonica variegata* is a slightly more difficult plant that will be inclined to have brown leaf edges if neglected. Larger plants of this variety will remain more compact and attractive if they are potted into standard John Innes No. 3 Potting Compost.

Before discussing the ivies I must mention a man-made plant, fatshedera, which gets its name from its two parents, fatsia and hedera. Having enlarged ivy-shaped leaves on an upright stem, the fatshedera is an excellent choice for the back row of a group of plants. *Fatshedera lizei variegata*, the variegated-leaved variety, is a more colourful plant, though inclined to have

brown leaf edges if the compost is kept permanently wet.

For those with an experimental turn of mind it will be interesting to try grafting one of the more decorative small-leaved hederas onto the top of a fatshedera, thus giving a fascinating plant that will never fail to interest acquaintances. To perform the grafting operation it will be necessary to have a reasonably healthy fatshedera plant about 3 to 4 ft. in height, which should have its growing tip removed. The stem should be attached to a cane to keep it erect. With a sharp knife cut down twice into the stem just above a leaf joint for about 1 in. Prepare four wedge-shaped ivy tip cuttings from firm pieces, and insert these into the cross-shaped cut made in the top of the fatshedera. Tie them very firmly in position with raffia or adhesive tape, place a polythene bag over them and tie the bag in position. The bag will prevent the cuttings drying out and will consequently help them to bond much more readily. When the cuttings begin to grow the bag must be

31

removed, and when the ivy pieces have developed several new leaves the tips should be pinched out to encourage a bushy appearance.

Hederas (Ivies)

In spite of flowering plants, exotic foliaged ones, and new introductions, the hederas, or ivies, still retain their popularity, and can well form an interesting

specialised collection of plants. In fact, a collection of ivies would give a pleasing display all the year round. There are about 25 different kinds to choose from, though only about 15 would be readily available.

We hear many opinions to the contrary, but it has been my experience that all the ivies offered for sale as house plants also make excellent garden plants. Success in establishing them out of doors depends to some extent on the planting time. Give the soil time to warm up, then, about the middle of May, plant them out. On walls, in the rock garden, or dotted around in the shrub border they will be a continual source of pleasure. By far the most spectacular is *Hedera canariensis* and, when planted against a sheltered wall, there can be few climbing plants that give a better year-round display. Some I planted a few years ago were reluctant to produce anything more than the odd bit of straggling growth until two substantial York paving stones were placed on the soil immediately in front of them. The cool, moist root run under the stones seemed to be exactly what the doctor ordered. Grown in this way there should never be any shortage of cream and green material for floral arranging.

Even when the last spark of life appears to have deserted your ivy, put it in the garden instead of the bin – the results, nine times out of ten, will surprise you.

But the subject is indoor plants, to which I return. Of the larger leaved ivies probably *H. canariensis* and *H. maculata* are the most popular; others, such as the varieties Ravenholst and Gold Leaf, have fallen out of favour. Indoors, ivies all require similar conditions for success – the most important being a light, airy room and a modest temperature in the region of 55°F. (13°C.) Hot and dry conditions encourage red spider mites, and the browning of leaf edges is by way of being their trade mark.

Almost all growers of house plants list a good selection of hederas, so there would not seem to be any need for repeating them all here. However, some of my particular favourites are worthy of special mention.

Hedera helix Adam has grey-green variegation and tiny leaves which are perfectly shaped and compactly arranged on the stem, to the point where they overlap on particularly good specimens. Because of the tightly matted leaves, care must be taken not to get the centre of the plant too wet, or wet at all for that matter. It will also pay to periodically check over the plants and remove any dead leaves that would be liable to rot if left in the centre. The compact leaves and distinct variegation make this variety a great favourite with the florists for adding the final touch to brides' bouquets.

The easily grown *H. canariensis* is quite the best of those with bolder leaves. One of its drawbacks is its unwillingness to branch when the growing tip is removed. Instead, it continues to grow from the leaf bud immediately below the position where the tip was taken out. So, in order to keep the plant within bounds, the growth should be wound back and forth around itself. When twisting the stems, take the simple precaution of bending them in a gentle arch, for if the growth is arranged at too acute an angle the flow of sap

Plants grouped together on a table often seem
to benefit by their proximity to one another. If
the table is glass topped it is particularly
suitable as any water which may be spilt does
no damage

Opposite: Hedera Jubilee, sometimes known as
Golden Heart on account of the gold centre to
the leaves

Right: Cyclamen Silver Leaf, a recent introduction with distinctive leaf colouring, and the
Creeping Fig, *Ficus pumila*

Opposite: Wrought-iron stands are usually sympathetic to foliage plants. Shown here, from top: *Hedera helix* Adam, *Begonia masoniana* and *Chlorophytum capense variegatum*

A standard ivy, *Hedera* Little Diamond, made by grafting this ivy onto a fatshedera rootstock

is checked and the part beyond the fractured stem invariably dies off.

Stocks of the variety Little Diamond vary considerably in quality, so care must be taken when making one's selection to ensure that the individual leaves are, as the name suggests, diamond shaped. Good stock should also have naturally twisting stems, and such plants are particularly suitable for grafting on top of fatshedera, as described on p. 31.

I am including the variety Glacier not so much for its attractiveness as for its lasting qualities. For inclusion in an arrangement of plants, to trail over the edge of the container and break its line, Glacier is ideal. It is also particularly suitable for use as a trailing plant in window-boxes out of doors and does not seem to mind harsh weather.

The small-leaved ivies almost all branch freely when the growing tips have been removed; this should be done occasionally to keep the plants compact and tidy. One of the exceptions is Jubilee (commonly named Golden Heart on account of its gold-centred leaves with a green perimeter), and for this reason it is not often grown commercially. In full sun in the rock garden, however, it can be relied upon to give a good year-round display, for although there is a tendency to wander, growth is easily snipped back and kept under control.

THE PINEAPPLE OR BROMELIAD FAMILY

Named after the Swedish botanist, Bromel, members of the *Bromeliaceae*, the Pineapple Family, are much neglected. If only on account of their durability, they deserve to be more popular.

A problem here was trying to decide whether the bromeliads should be included among the flowering plants or the foliage plants, but as most of them take several years to produce flowers (some as many as fifteen) I feel that they are with us longer as foliage rather than as flowering plants, and have included them in this chapter.

Beginning with the smallest members of the family, there are the cryptanthuses and tillandsias, the latter having an exciting range of bract shapes, and flowers – mostly in shades of blue – that are short-lived. For the bottle garden there can be no better choice than the compact cryptanthuses that can remain undisturbed for long periods without attention. These are grown primarily for their colouring, and, perhaps more particularly, for their fascinating shapes that have earned for them the apt common name of Earth Stars.

The flowers of the cryptanthuses are, on the whole, insignificant and barely emerge from the tightly overlapping leaves of the plants. In common with other members of the family, offsets will be produced at soil level when flowering has finished. When large enough these offsets can be removed, by bending them to one side, and be planted up individually in small pots filled with a peaty mixture. There will be a marked lessening in the time taken for these to root if the pots are stood on a bed of peat which has an electric soil-

Cryptanthuses, members of the Bromeliad Family can be grown on logs, as shown, or on pieces of bark suspended from the ceiling as mobiles. *C. tricolor* is displayed on the lower part of the log and the mottled-leaved *C. fosterianus* above it

warming cable running through it.

Cryptanthus tricolor

Cryptanthus tricolor, unfortunately rather a costly plant, is of striking appearance, particularly when the cream and green striped leaves take on a reddish tint. Both the colouring and appearance of *C. tricolor* is greatly improved when the plants are grown in a natural way on an old log or piece of bark, instead of in the more conventional pot. These 'mobiles', as they are called, have a certain fascination when suspended in mid-air on a length of clear nylon fishing line. Only close inspection will convince admirers that the 'object' is not floating in space.

Mobiles are easily made by knocking plants from their pots and placing a wad of fresh sphagnum moss around the exposed roots; the moss ball is then tied securely to the chosen anchorage. Nails can be driven into the bark or log and used for tying the plants, and these can subsequently be concealed by an additional bit of moss wedged in around them. Needless to say, mobiles are better suited to the greenhouse or conservatory where drips resulting from watering will not be a problem. Water the plants by saturating the moss with a fine syringe when necessary, or by plunging the plant and anchorage in a bucket of tepid water.

Some of the tillandsias will also be perfectly happy if attached to a log in this way, though care must be exercised to ensure that only those with small, compact rosettes are selected.

Larger Bromeliads

Space permits mention of only three of the larger bromeliads, *Aechmea rhodocyanea*, *Neoregelia carolinae tricolor* and *Vriesia splendens*. All are spectacular plants that should give little difficulty if a minimum temperature of 60°F. (16°C.) can be maintained.

Aechmea rhodocyanea is a very fine plant, and one that the uninformed look at with amazement as they exclaim 'Is it real?' They might well ask, for a mature plant with a well-developed flowering bract has few competitors in the 'exotic honours' field. Large, straplike, recurving leaves, banded in light and dark shades of grey, form an urn-shaped rosette, the centre of which must be kept topped up with water. From the centre of the 'urn' the bold pink bract emerges, and from the bract strikingly blue flowers eventually appear. The cost of these plants is often bemoaned by the would-be purchaser, but it should be borne in mind that they very rarely take less than four years to produce a bract. With the assistance of carefully measured chemicals and gases, plants can be induced to flower in less time; the results, however, rarely match up to the naturally produced product.

Ideally, aechmeas should be purchased when the bract is a little above the water level in the urn. Records show that, when purchased at this stage, it is quite possible for them to remain colourful for up to 12 months. As the bract begins to fade and die, so, too, does the rosette from which it came; this is common to all bromeliads. When the main rosette is no longer attractive it should be cut away with a sharp knife, care being taken not to damage the new young shoots that will by then be sprouting from the base of the parent plant.

Vriesia fenestralis, **an extremely handsome bromeliad, with light green leaves intricately marked with darker green. This is a difficult plant to grow, but it is well worth the extra effort required**

Much is said about whether or not one should remove these shoots and pot them up individually, or leave them to develop still attached to the parent rosette. I can only quote the experience of a keen gardener of my acquaintance, who was in fact the part-time gardener at my local railway station. He left the cluster of five 'pups' on his plant, and two years later he had the most magnificent specimen with four heads at the peak of perfection, and all in full colour at the same time. What is more, they were still in the same soil. Why did number five fail to develop? There is always a 'why' in gardening!

In the greenhouse, healthy plants will produce side growths that develop quickly and may have bracts in as little as one year, but this is the exception and two years at least must normally be allowed.

With all larger bromeliads it is important that the 'urn' be kept topped up with water, preferably clean rain water which should be completely changed periodically to prevent it becoming stagnant.

Neoregelia carolinae tricolor is another spectacular and thoroughly reliable plant which I first saw growing in an airport restaurant where the amount of natural daylight was almost nil. In fact, the neoregelia was one of only two survivors from the original planting – this in spite of the fact that the 'urn' seemed to provide a convenient receptacle for discarded cigarette ends.

The saw-edged overlapping leaves will brighten any display with their cream and green variegation; strong sunlight will give an overall russet flush to the leaves. Mature plants eventually have bright red centres, and at the same time the rather insignificant flowering bract appears in the middle of the urn, barely emerging from the water that must always be present. A word of caution, as the flowers appear the water in the urn takes on an unpleasant odour and should be changed more frequently than usual. The compost in the pot must be kept moist, but never saturated. Many of the bromeliads will tolerate comparatively dry root conditions provided the water level in the urn is maintained, but the lower leaves of the neoregelia become brown and shrivelled if the soil is excessively dry for any length of time.

The vriesias include some of the most interesting plants in the family. In particular there are *Vriesia hieroglyphica* and *V. fenestralis*, both of which have astonishingly intricate leaf markings. These I mention only by way of interest, knowing that they are difficult to acquire, and that only the true expert could ever hope to succeed with them indoors.

Vriesia splendens is a plant that is generally available and relatively easy to care for. It should have a light position in the room. An interesting feature of this plant is the way in which the transverse light and dark bands of colour on the leaves gradually blend into a greenish-brown overall colouring as the spear-shaped red bract increases in size. Well-grown specimen plants may have bracts up to 2 ft. in length.

Bromeliads, on the whole, have rather poor root systems, so when potting it is important to ensure that a light, open compost is used. One successful mixture consists of the following ingredients: one-third pine needles, one-third oak or birch leaf-mould, and one-third peat. If all those materials are not at hand, prepare a mixture which conforms to this specification as nearly as possible, bearing in mind the need for an open, spongy compost.

Vriesia splendens bearing its spear-like bract, the red colour of which contrasts strikingly with the brown and green horizontally striped leaves

Opposite: Zebrina pendula, with silver, grey, green and purple leaves

THE SPIDERWORT FAMILY

The *Commelinaceae* or Spiderwort Family is native to tropical and subtropical regions and includes the tradescantias, which will be familiar to many readers.

Tradescantias

There is always a soft spot for one or other of the tradescantia tribe, first introduced to this country some 300 years ago and still as popular as ever. Most are easy to care for, while others are a wee bit difficult; almost all of them root like the proverbial weed when propagated from cuttings. For the beginner there can be no better choice than tradescantias, and the many varieties available · will ensure a pleasing range of colour throughout the year.

In the easier range there are the varieties Silver, Gold, *tricolor*, *purpurea* and the newer Quick Silver, which has altogether larger and more colourful leaves. *Zebrina pendula*, formerly named *Tradescantia zebrina*, with silver, green, purple and grey leaves, is another in the easy range. Slightly more difficult are *T. blossfeldiana variegata*, *T. quadricolor* and the related *Setcreasea purpurea*, the Purple Heart.

Many are the complaints we hear of tradescantias turning green in colour and losing their bright appearance; much of this is due to inadequate light and too much moisture at the roots. The old adage that tradescantias should be kept dry and starved in order to preserve the variegation has never proved itself in my experience; such treatment results in thin, weedy growth that may be variegated but is certainly never attractive. Stand them in the lightest possible window, feed them regularly and pot them on as required is the best advice for obtaining healthy and variegated plants. Also, when green shoots appear on the plant they should be ruthlessly removed, as these contain much more chlorophyll and so grow more rapidly, leading to a completely green plant in time.

One is often shown a tradescantia with the proud comment that the plant is four, five or even six years old; and, quite honestly, they almost all look as if they are at least that age. To get the best out of these plants,

new ones should be started each year in order to provide fresh, vigorous growth. Select the most colourful growths, about 4in. in length, and put five or six around the edge of a 3½-in. pot filled with John Innes No. 2 Potting Compost. Rooting them first in a normal propagating mixture is a complete waste of time. To keep the plants compact, the cuttings should have their growing tips removed almost as soon as they have rooted.

Where space permits, it may be worthwhile preparing a hanging basket of tradescantias. Do this by selecting half-a-dozen potfuls of the most colourful plants and space them out evenly in a basket that has been lined with black polythene and filled with John Innes No. 2 Potting Compost. It is important that the polythene should have several holes made in it so that excess water can drain away easily. Tie in some of the longer shoots underneath the basket and pinch out the growing tips periodically to improve the shape of the plant; and weed out those green shoots as they appear. The *tricolor* and Silver varieties make particularly good subjects for use in baskets.

THE DAISY FAMILY

The *Compositae* or Daisy Family provides us with many of our most colourful and adaptable garden plants, and the potential of many as pot plants has not been neglected. Both of the plants mentioned here are grown primarily for their foliage, as their flowers are comparatively insignificant.

Gynura sarmentosa

This plant attracts the eye, especially when the sunlight picks out the velvety purple colouring of the topmost leaves. Reasonably easy to grow, *Gynura sarmentosa* may in some conditions be genuinely described as rampant, though it will present problems when culture is at fault. It abhors wet conditions and seems to enjoy a warm, sunny position. As house plants go, this Dead Nettle is unusual in that it produces flowers, orange coloured, fairly freely. Alas, these are

Gynura sarmentosa, with its green and purple leaves, and unusual velvety texture

Tradescantia Quick Silver, which has larger and more colourful leaves than other varieties of this type. As can be seen, it is a splendid plant for a hanging basket

Below: Members of the tradescantia family, clockwise from bottom left-hand corner: *T. tricolor, T. purpurea, Zebrina pendula* (syn. *T. zebrina), T.* Quick Silver and *T. quadricolor*

in no way an attraction, and they should be removed while still in bud on account of their abominable odour. Cuttings are little trouble to root, so it is better to periodically propagate a few fresh young plants and to dispose of the older ones when the new have rooted.

Senecio macroglossa

Deceptive, in that it is frequently mistaken for an ivy, *Senecio macroglossa* is recognised as something different when one touches the thick, fleshy leaves. The shape of the leaf is more or less triangular, and the plant is a natural climber, twining itself around any convenient support. It is comparatively easy to please if given a light position and if the watering-can is used sparingly. Be particularly careful not to water freely during the winter months. The orange-coloured daisy flowers are attractive, but rather inconspicuous against the cream and green background of the foliage.

THE LILY FAMILY

The *Liliaceae* or Lily Family is known to everybody and, like many other plant families, it includes subjects which bear little superficial resemblance to each other. Such is Mother Nature's way that if a sansevieria plant is placed next to a hyacinth in flower, the uninitiated would find it difficult to believe that they are botanically related. However, see *Sansevieria trifasciata laurentii* in flower in mid-summer and the similarity is immediately made clear. The pale green, faintly scented flowers

Aspidistra lurida, the Cast Iron Plant, which as the author says, is 'the toughie to outlast all toughies'

Below: Remarkably like an ivy, *Senecio macroglossa* has thick, fleshy, cream and green foliage and is a natural climber

Chlorophytum capense variegatum, the ever popular Spider Plant

of this sansevieria are frequently looked upon as something of a phenomena, but they are, in fact, quite freely produced on mature plants. Occasionally the small sansevieria will also oblige with a flower and the owner may with some justification feel that his plant deserves more than a passing glance.

Aspidistra lurida

The Cast Iron Plant, *Aspidistra lurida,* is the toughie to outlast all toughies, and there is a keen desire by many to see the return of the aspidistra to the nurseryman's list. Sad to say, the aspidistra, besides being durable, is also lamentably slow growing when compared to the more modern house plant. The cost of growing them today would be prohibitive and beyond the purse of most would-be purchasers.

When I asked an old gardener how he cared for his 60-year-old Cast Iron Plant that was glowing with good health, he supplied the following rather surprising answer: 'Every springtime I knock it out of its pot, remove about one-third of the soil (roots and all) from the lower part of the root ball. Then I put a crock over the hole in the bottom of the pot, add an equivalent amount of soil to that which was removed from the root ball, and place the plant on top of it. After watering in, the plant never looks back.' Drastic, but effective.

Chlorophytum capense variegatum

The common name for this plant is the Spider Plant. It is another of our friendly house plants that can be propagated without difficulty. Grass-like in appearance, chlorophytums produce plantlets on long stalks that can be rooted in ordinary soil by pegging them down in much the same way as one would layer a strawberry runner. Plants are sometimes reluctant to produce these little ones but it has been my experience that, when large enough, all chlorophytums produce young plantlets, and very fine they are when seen trailing from a hanging basket. For success, keep them well watered, well fed, and pot them on into slightly larger containers annually in the spring. Other than that, all they ask for is a light position and a moderate temperature. Browning of the leaf tips presents a minor problem, and is usually caused when plants are

41

Sansevieria trifasciata laurentii, a popular house plant which is usually referred to by its common name – Mother-in-Law's Tongue

Maranta leuconeura erythrophylla; the bright green leaves have attractive red and brown markings

inadequately fed or are in need of potting on.

Sansevieria trifasciata laurentii

Mother-in-Law's Tongue, as it is called, is a plant that seems to thrive on neglect, and it is decidedly happier when the soil is very much on the dry side, particularly in winter. Cold or wet conditions or a combination of the two are the worst enemies of this plant, but it will thrive in warm, sunny situations.

When purchasing, it is wise to select plants that have young shoots growing up at the side of the pot; one can then be reasonably sure that they are well established.

As the rhizomes increase in both size and number they will break the pot in which they are growing, be it clay or plastic, and this is a positive sign that the plant is in need of fresh soil around the roots. Use John Innes No. 2 Potting Compost and pot firmly. As older plants tend to become top-heavy it is wise to use heavier clay pots rather than plastic pots when potting.

THE MARANTA FAMILY

It would be bold and foolish of me to include the entire maranta tribe – members of the *Marantaceae* – in this easily-grown section, but there are two that seem to qualify – *Maranta leuconeura kerchoveana* and *M. leuconeura erythrophylla.*

Maranta leuconeura kerchoveana

On reading the above heading one cannot help but feel that common names are, in their way, something of a blessing. For good measure this plant has two: Rabbit's Tracks, which it gets from the smudged brown spots on the attractive green leaf, and Prayer Plant. The reason for the second name is not so obvious until the leaves are seen to fold up together (like hands in prayer) as darkness descends. This is a somewhat eerie sight when first seen by torchlight in a darkened greenhouse; leaves that were perfectly flat during the day having folded together showing only their reverse sides. One gets the feeling that every movement one makes is being watched!

Maranta leuconeura erythrophylla

Though *Maranta leuconeura erythrophylla* does not appear to have a common name, it surely cannot be long before a less tongue-twisting alternative is found for the average housewife. Understandably enough, this plant is sometimes sold as *Maranta tricolor.* It is a particularly exciting plant that has come on the scene only in the past few years. At first sight the predominantly brown leaves, with quite fantastic stripes and patterns running through them, suggests a delicate stove (very warm greenhouse) type of plant. Limited experience

43

has shown that it propagates readily, and is more durable than almost any other plant in the entire family. However, do not run away with the idea that it is a tradescantia type of plant; it will require a minimum temperature of at least 65°F. (18°C.) and careful watering for success. When potting marantas, the addition of extra leaf-mould or peat to recommended composts is essential, and it should be firmed lightly. Exposure to strong, direct sunlight for any length of time should be avoided, as it will quickly result in the leaves losing their colour and the plant taking on a generally hard appearance.

THE MULBERRY FAMILY

The members of the *Moraceae* – it is a large family containing 55 genera – are mostly native to the tropics. In this, the Mulberry Family, as it is commonly called, I am concerned only with the genus *Ficus* (the Figs), a collection of plants of considerable importance to the house plant enthusiast.

Ficuses

The Rubber Plant, *Ficus elastica decora*, has, over the years, become something of a symbol in the house plant section of horticulture. It would be virtually impossible to answer here all the questions that are asked about Rubber Plants, unless many other house plants were to be excluded from the chapter. Also, since so many different species of ficus are cultivated in the home, I have decided to give general information on ficus culture rather than a catalogued list of ficus names with specific cultural instructions.

Of all the questions that are asked, the most frequent is, without doubt, the one concerning loss of leaves. When plants lose their lower leaves it is, in most cases, due to overwatering, although it is quite natural for older plants to shed leaves as they increase in height. During the winter months water should be given sparingly as the plants are dormant and, therefore, need much less moisture. Rapid defoliation suggests other possible causes, such as overfeeding; insecticides used incorrectly; the use of harmful oil-based leaf-cleaning agents applied too frequently or at excessive strength; or gas fumes.

Considerable harm is also done by potting plants at the wrong time of the year, or when, in fact, potting is unnecessary. The layman is frequently misled into feeling that the obvious answer to the appearance of yellow lower leaves is to purchase a larger pot and transfer his ailing plant to it. Potting on (in effect, removing the plant from one pot and putting it into a pot one size larger) and disturbing roots that are probably damaged anyway, is a positive way of writing the plant's death warrant. Sick plants should be carefully nursed back to health by placing them in a draught-free corner where an even temperature of about 65°F. (18°C.) can be maintained. Above all, water must be given sparingly to give new roots an opportunity to get on the move.

Some ficus owners are plagued by their plants losing leaves, while others are casting worried glances at the top of the plant as it makes its way inexorably towards the ceiling. It was at one time a standing joke to suggest cutting a hole in the ceiling so that the plant could also be admired in the bedroom above!

For plants that are getting too tall and running out of head-room, one of three solutions is suggested. First, ask your nurseryman if he will be prepared to accept it in exchange for a smaller one, with suitable cash adjustment, naturally. Secondly, consider lopping off the top of the plant – probably a more practical suggestion. Do this by using sharp secateurs to cut straight through the main stem about 1in. above a leaf joint at the height you wish your plant to be. The cut will exude latex that will dry up in time or it may be sealed by rubbing it over with a little moist clay soil, or ordinary compost. The plant will subsequently produce four or five new shoots from the topmost leaf joints, so giving it the appearance of a standard specimen, like, say, a standard rose or fuchsia.

The third suggestion is for the more adventurous, and involves an operation known as air-layering. For this, one should have to hand the following items: a sharp knife, a 2-ft. cane, two handfuls of wet sphagnum moss, a piece of polythene about 8in. by 6in. (one of the stouter polythene bags slit down the side and along the bottom is suitable), string, a piece of matchstick and someone to assist with the operation. Begin by removing a leaf at the height you wish your plant to be. Follow this by getting your helper to hold the stem in position while you cut halfway through the main stem about 1 in. below the joint from which the leaf was removed. Then bend the stem carefully, and very slightly so that the knife can be turned to make an upward cut through the actual node. (The flow of latex will do no harm, though care should be taken not to get it on one's clothing, as such stains are difficult to remove). Insert the piece of matchstick in the cut to hold it open, then dust with one of the hormone rooting powders. The cane should now be tied in position above and below the cut mark in the form of a splint and inserted in the pot. This will obviate the possibility of the stem keeling over and breaking off.

The wet moss is then placed on either side of the cut mark and tied in position. Wrap the moss around with the polythene and tie it tightly above and below the moss. After some six to eight weeks, when a plentiful supply of white roots can be seen inside the polythene, use secateurs to sever the rooted section just below the moss ball. Allow the severed end to dry, and carefully remove the polythene before potting the plant into a peaty compost, with the moss ball intact. The compost is watered in to settle it down and is then kept on the dry side until the plant is obviously seen to be growing away in the mixture, when normal watering can begin.

The remaining lower portion of the plant will then produce shoots from the topmost leaf joints, but, in the process, it is usual for the plant to shed some of its lower leaves.

The foregoing information applies to healthy Rub-

Ficus elastica decora, the Rubber Plant, which is probably the most popular of all house plants

ber Plants, and one should not be too optimistic when treating ailing plants in this way.

Indoors, the Rubber Plant has a growing season that extends, more or less, from March through to October, during which time it will put on an average of one leaf per month – many more where conditions are favourable. However, some plants will go through the entire summer and develop no new leaves at all, and for no apparent reason. Occasionally, if the plant suffers a setback it will stop growing for a time; until, in fact, conditions are again to its liking. At these times it is particularly important to ensure that the winter watering procedure is practised, that is, giving water only when it is obviously required.

Temperature is quite important if plants are to develop leaves of normal size; over 65°F. (18°C.) the leaves will be larger than normal and inclined to droop, under 45°F. (7°C.) much smaller leaves will result. Plants that have been subjected to widely fluctuating temperatures will show this by producing large or small leaves, depending upon the temperature prevailing at the time these leaves were about to open.

THE PEPPER FAMILY

This family, the *Piperaceae*, contains a group of plants known as peperomias. There are many different species and varieties, the majority of which are compact and low growing. Those with variegated leaves need ample light in order to retain their attractive colouring while those with darker leaves become hard in appearance when exposed to excessive sunlight.

The Best-Known Peperomias

Best known of the peperomias are *Peperomia magnoliae-folia*, with fleshy leaves, cream and green in colour; *P. hederaefolia,* with metallic grey leaves; and the

Opposite: The leaves of *Peperomia sandersii,* with dark stripes of green on a grey background, have an almost luminous quality

Two other peperomias, *P. rotundifolia* and *P. tithymaloides* (in foreground). The rounded pottery container is especially well suited to their habit and leaf formation, giving the impression, almost, of a flower arrangement

Left to right: *Peperomia hederaefolia,* with metallic grey leaves; *P. scandens,* a variegated trailing species, and *P. caperata,* a species with dark green leaves

Right: An enthusiast's growing case in which house plants are grown in controlled environments. Plants which have special requirements with regard to temperature, light or humidity can be grown to perfection in such cases

attractive dark green, crinkle-leaved species, *P. caperata.* The last two are not difficult to propagate if this is done in much the same way as described for saint-paulias (see p. 115), by using single leaves.

With the variegated sorts it is necessary to take a cutting with part of the stem attached to the leaf if a variegated plant is to result from the propagation. Cuttings prepared from leaves only will result in green growth. Yet the leaves of *P. sandersii,* with dark stripes of green on a grey background, can be propagated by cutting the leaf into sections, and the resultant growth is invariably identical to the parent leaf in both colour and pattern.

Trailing Peperomias

Three trailing peperomias, ideal for edging plant troughs and containers, are *P. scandens, P. glabella variegata* and the more recently introduced *P. tithymaloides,* which has mottled green and gold variegations. The latter produces occasional green shoots that are not unattractive and, indeed, help to set off the variegation. No more than three or four green pieces need be left, as any more would quickly outgrow the more colourful pieces.

Peperomia rotundifolia is the most recent to be tried as a house plant. It has plain green, rather uninteresting leaves, but it has an advantage over most indoor plants in that it regularly produces its clean, white flowers. When the flowers fade, cut back to a sound pair of leaves, so that fresh growth may be encouraged.

Pilea cadierei, called the Aluminium Plant because of the colour of the markings on its shapely small leaves

Opposite: A beautifully maintained indoor 'garden' in which a young specimen of *Monstera deliciosa borsigiana* forms the focal point. Ficus, sansevieria, maranta, peperomias and Ivies keep it company

THE PROTEA FAMILY

The *Proteaceae* or Protea Family is a large group of plants containing many large shrubs, which were particularly popular over 100 years ago when large conservatories were fashionable and could provide the plants with the protection that most of them require.

Grevillea robusta

Here again we have two common names for the same plant – the Australian Wattle and the Silk Oak. It is a fast-growing green plant, that quickly adapts itself to most reasonable growing conditions. It is easily reared from seed, and besides being an attractive indoor plant it plays an important part as the centre-piece of bedding schemes in many public parks during the summer months.

Rapid growth is a drawback in some respects, as grevilleas will outgrow their headroom in a matter of two or three years, if conditions are to their liking. Ideally, by the time it reaches the ceiling the keen house plant grower should have a younger plant growing on, ready to take the place of the larger one. It is not everyone who has the heart to destroy over-grown, healthy plants, so finding a suitable home for the monster becomes a problem. The garage showroom, or the hotel manager will often take these off your hands and give them a home where overhead space is improved by the presence of the Silk Oak.

49

comparatively easy to care for, and only when the compost is well filled with roots are they inclined to become hard in appearance and less attractive. Like tradescantias, they are simple to propagate, so it should be the rule to periodically raise new plants from fresh cuttings. Regular pinching out of the growing tips is a 'must' if growth is not to become leggy.

THE VINE FAMILY

A characteristic of the Vine Family or *Vitaceae* is that the majority of the members of the family are climbers and produce tendrils which help them to attach themselves to supports.

Cissus antarctica and Rhoicissus rhomboidea

The two important contributions made by the Vine Family to present-day house plant displays are the Kangaroo Vine, *Cissus antarctica,* and the Grape Ivy, *Rhoicissus rhomboidea.* The first-mentioned is reasonably easy under most conditions, though it does not approve of hot, dry rooms, particularly if the compost in the pot is allowed to become too dry. Under these conditions, the leaves take on a crisp, dry appearance, and the plant does not recover very readily. Yet its close relative, the Grape Ivy (there is also the larger-leaved *Rhoicissus rhomboidea* Jubilee) is probably the most durable of all indoor plants. Of climbing habit, it has naturally glossy leaves.

THE STRAWBERRY FAMILY

The *Saxifragaceae* or Strawberry Family is well known to everyone. The production of new plants from runners is a characteristic of this family, and is clearly shown in the house plant member of the family.

Saxifraga sarmentosa

Saxifraga sarmentosa, an attractive trailing plant with small pink and white flowers, makes rapid growth, and ease of propagation ensures that it will retain its popularity. Mother of Thousands, as it is called, is seen to best advantage when placed in a pot or small orchid-type slatted-wood basket and suspended from the window lintel. Small plantlets snipped from the parent plant establish themselves readily.

THE NETTLE FAMILY

The botanical name for the Nettle Family is the *Urticaceae.* In the economic world, hops probably provide the best known example of this family.

Pileas

The Nettle Family's two main contributions to the modern house plant scene are the attractive variegated plants *Pilea cadierei* and *P. cadierei minima.* The latter is rapidly gaining in popularity over its larger-leaved forbear. With aluminium-coloured leaves (hence the common name of Aluminium Plant), these are

Opposite, top: Saxifraga sarmentosa, a pretty plant for suspending from a window lintel or ceiling so that the little plantlets dangle below

Opposite: Cissus antarctica, which is adaptable to most conditions but dislikes hot, dry rooms

Above: Rhoicissus rhomboidea, perhaps the toughest of all modern house plants

Ficus elastica tricolor, a variety of the common Rubber Plant with pink, cream and green leaves. It is, however, rather more difficult to grow than its common counterpart

Right: The ornamental grass *Acorus gramineus variegatus, Ficus pumila* and a stately codiaeum (croton) grouped in a container

Chapter 5
Unusual House Plants

When gathering together a collection of plants it is wise to include a few that are out of the ordinary, be it for their flowers, leaf colour, or simply because they have an unusual shape. Since unusual and difficult are almost synonymous for many house plants, beginners in particular must be careful when making their selection. They should bear in mind the thought that it is much more pleasing to see a comparatively ordinary plant prosper than to see the rapid decline of a more colourful and unusual one. There is little doubt that a well-grown ivy or philodendron is much more attractive than an exotic plant that has been reduced to a bare stem with two stubborn leaves valiantly hanging on at the top – probably hoping for better days to come!

Acorus gramineus variegatus

Of the grassy-foliaged plants available, the golden-leaved acorus is one of the best, being compact, colourful and easy to grow. With almost any house plant it would be fatal if it were allowed to stand in water for any length of time, but the acorus is rarely too wet, and will often do better if the pot is partly submerged in water. It is a particularly fine plant for a bottle garden (see p. 88).

Aglaonemas

In the past few months I have been agreeably sur-

An interesting new aglaonema, Silver Queen,
a compact variety with silver-grey leaves

Opposite: Araucaria excelsa, **the Norfolk Island
Pine is a plant which is now returning to favour.
It has a fresh green appearance with graceful
branches radiating from the central stem**

prised at the way in which a plant of *Aglaonema pseudo-bracteatum* has tolerated indifferent treatment and the smoky atmosphere of a club bar. In its favour, no doubt, is the constant minimum temperature of 63°F. (17°C.) that is maintained for 24 hours a day. Aglaonemas are difficult to purchase, but there seems to be much interest in the new variety Silver Queen, which is short and compact with silver-grey leaves and which is likely to become more plentiful in time.

Mealy bug is a troublesome pest that is difficult to eradicate and it will attack the roots as well as the leaves. A thorough drenching with malathion insecticide is effective if the bug is detected in time.

Aralia elegantissima

Belonging to the same family as the hederas, or ivies, *Aralia elegantissima* is, however, a much more trying plant to care for, wet and cold conditions reducing it to a bare stalk in a very short space of time. A temperature of 65°F. (18°C.) is required for successful cultivation, the soil being kept moist, but never saturated. Surprisingly enough it adapts itself very well to the modern technique of capillary watering,

which simply means that plant pots are placed on a bed of sand that is kept permanently wet. Plastic pots are used when plants are watered in this way as the thin base permits the compost in the pot and the sand to come into direct contact.

Mature plants of eight years or more in age lose much of their fine-leaved, elegant appearance as they develop into small trees, the leaves becoming much coarser and larger in the process. There is little fear of having them push the roof off indoors though, as growth becomes much slower, and even the expert would have difficulty in keeping plants for more than a few years.

Araucaria excelsa

The Norfolk Island Pine, *Araucaria excelsa*, popular in the past, is slowly coming back into favour. In common with many of the Victorian potted plants, it is slow growing and therefore, by definition, costly. In a cool room, where the temperature need not exceed 50°F. (10°C.), its tiered green leaves seldom fail to please. Water moderately, as the leaves quickly lose their crisp appearance if the compost is permanently wet;

likewise, leaves are spoilt if the temperature is excessive. It is usual for new plants to be raised from seed, but it is a slow business. Sow seed in John Innes No. 1 Potting Compost in February or March.

Begonias

Of the begonias, the *rex* types, with their intricate and colourful leaf patterns, are the best known. For indoor use, I find that some varieties of *Begonia rex* are better than others and, in particular, those with smaller leaves are easier to care for. After a time plants become unsightly when the rhizomatous growth extends beyond the edge of the pot, and lower leaves are lost in the process. Although it presents considerable difficulty, I have known enthusiasts to succeed when attempting to root leaf cuttings in pans of moist peat on a window-sill. Firm, unmarked leaves are cut up into small pieces a little larger than a postage stamp, then placed on moist peat with the coloured side uppermost. It is important that the compost should only be moist; if it is too wet the cuttings will rot, while if it is too dry they will shrivel up. (As a rough guide to moistness, one should be just able to squeeze moisture from the peat, or compost, when a fistful is tightly compressed). Cover the pot with a small piece of glass (turn it daily) and keep the temperature at around 65°F. (18°C.). Direct sunlight on the cuttings will be damaging, but a light position must be provided, and additional artificial light in the evening will be an advantage. About six weeks will elapse before the first tiny leaves appear.

Besides the *rex* types there are many other equally interesting and attractive fibrous-rooted begonias, and one finds it difficult to understand why these delightful plants are not more popular. The humble green ivies are bought in huge numbers yet a serious attempt to popularise plants of the *B. corolicta*, *B. daedalea* and *B. mazae* types met with utter failure some years ago. Perhaps the public distrusted their fine foliage and exotic blooms. My experience suggests that these suspicions are quite unfounded, as I have successfully grown a selection of fibrous begonias over the years and find them less demanding than many of the house plants normally placed in the 'easy' category.

At present the majority are in short supply, and so are difficult to acquire, but I feel that in time these plants will be given a second chance by the nurseryman, and they will then be more readily accepted by more knowledgeable and adventurous house plant enthusiasts.

Some, such as *B. fuchsioides*, *B. lucerna* and *B. corolicta* become too large for the average room in time, but they almost all propagate with ridiculous ease, so there is no difficulty in starting a few fresh plants. All must have ample feeding when they are established, and potting on into larger containers should be made a spring chore.

Slightly more difficult to propagate than the *B. rex* varieties, *B. masoniana* (known as Iron Cross) is, however, a superior plant, both in respect of durability and usefulness. With its distinctive Iron Cross marking in the centre of each leaf, it is particularly easy to use in small bowl arrangements, and equally useful for blending with other plants in larger displays.

Begonia masoniana, also known as Iron Cross, is one of the finest of its kind

Gynura sarmentosa, an introduction from Java
which can be rampant when it is given the
conditions it likes: warmth and good light are
its main requirements

A corner arrangement of house plants designed to create a nice balance and a variety of interest from the Rubber Plant (far right) to the small, red-spathed anthurium, the codiaeum and tradescantia in the terra-cotta container and the tall variegated ivy on the extreme left

Left: A saintpaulia and trailing ivy in a dolphin vase; such a combination of plants would make an attractive adornment for a sideboard or low table

House plants, for obvious reasons, should be used with discretion in bathrooms, but a few plants carefully placed can look extremely attractive. Shown here are *Fatshedera lizei variegata* and *Rhoicissus rhomboidea*

Peperomia glabella variegata, a useful plant for edging plant troughs and containers or indeed for any position where it can trail attractively

Caladiums

These aroids, available in many colours, have the most delicate foliage of all indoor plants. Indeed, the leaves of the most popular kind, *Caladium candidum*, are almost transparent, yet it is one of the easiest to care for indoors. Last year I tried one for the first time, and felt I had had full value when it lasted for four-and-a-half months – in an unheated room at that.

Corms are started into growth in warm peat beds in the greenhouse in the early part of the year, and the plants are on sale from the end of April. When the leaves die back naturally in the autumn one should be able, in theory, to allow the compost to dry before storing the corm in a minimum temperature of 60°F. (16°C.) until February, when the compost is gradually given more water to encourage fresh growth. This I have done, and I await results but am not too hopeful, knowing that it can be difficult to overwinter caladiums in a greenhouse where the conditions would seem to be almost ideal.

My plant responded to a watering programme that allowed the soil to dry a little between bouts with the watering-can. When a plant has been purchased, it will be advisable to support the larger leaves with thin canes, as they become top heavy and the petioles bend very easily, so restricting the flow of sap to the leaves and causing them to die.

As an experiment, this begonia has been grown for three years in Sorbo rubber (see p.102 for details), but this is not recommended as a practical alternative to compost

Below: An attractive variety of *Begonia rex* with silver foliage

Curiously complementary in their beautiful leaf markings are *Calathea ornata sanderiana* (left) and *Peperomia sandersii*. These would be in sympathy with ultra-modern room décors

Another calathea, *C. insignis* (left), with dark green markings on the pale green leaves, which have contrasting purple undersides, and *Maranta picturata*, whose light grey leaves with dark green margins are coloured maroon on the undersides

Calatheas

Many calatheas are difficult indoors, and some downright impossible. Probably the easiest is *Calathea louisae*, which has less colourful leaves than many of the others. *C. insignis* and *C. ornata sanderiana* are both very striking plants that will catch the eye in any collection. These, however, should be treated as being expendable and not be expected to live for more than a year or two at the most. Calatheas will not tolerate direct sunlight at any cost; and warm, humid conditions must be the aim when caring for them.

Comparatively slow growth and difficulty of culture tends to make calatheas costly and scarce.

Citrus mitis

Citrus mitis is a winner all the way, but it can be somewhat aggravating to see yellow, chlorotic leaves develop – as they often do – when the correct cultural needs of the plant have been supplied to the letter. The Calamondin Orange, as it is commonly called, is short and compact, without the spines normally associated with citrus plants. It has the considerable advantage over *C. sinensis*, the more common species, of bearing fruit on comparatively small plants.

In America these dwarf oranges are extremely popular, and to encourage sales the story goes that no cocktail bar is complete without its real live orange tree from which oranges can be plucked and used for flavouring. Having seen both, it would seem that the American product is very much better than our home-reared plants; success across the Atlantic owing much to the abundant sunshine available in California for ripening one-year-old wood that will bear fruit the following year. It will, therefore, be seen that providing the plants with the maximum amount of sunshine

Opposite: The Calamondin Orange, *Citrus mitis* with fruits like tangerine oranges. It needs plenty of sunshine to flower and fruit well

Codiaeum reidii — one of the finest pot plants in cultivation. The lovely patterned leaves are predominantly orange-pink in colour

during the summer months, when they can be put outside, is one way of encouraging them to flower and fruit. Guard against overwatering, as the weak root system quickly dies in wet conditions. Cuttings root with little difficulty, and these will sometimes fruit as little as 12 months from potting. The fruits resemble tangerine oranges and peel in much the same way, but are somewhat bitter.

Codiaeums (Crotons)

There seems to be no limit to the range and variety of colours to be found in codiaeum (croton) leaves, and these colours will improve considerably if the plants are exposed to the maximum amount of light available. In common with most plants of ornamental appearance, the codiaeum is a stove (very warm greenhouse) subject, so it must have an adequate temperature – 65°F. (18°C.) or more. Both low temperatures and dry conditions will result in leaf drop and the soil need only be very dry on one occasion for leaves to fall a week or two later.

Keep feeding codiaeums while they are actively

growing, and pot them on annually into slightly larger containers; John Innes No. 2 Potting Compost, well firmed, is the growing mixture to use. Red spider mite is a troublesome pest and a watchful eye (assisted by a magnifying glass) should be kept on the underside of leaves for signs of its presence.

Codiaeum reidii is recognised by keen plantsmen as one of the finest pot plants at present in cultivation. Mature specimens, growing in ideal greenhouse conditions, may have leaves as much as 18in. in length and 9in. across. These leaves are beautifully patterned and are predominantly orange-pink in colour. Not easy to grow indoors, it will, however, be well worth purchasing, if only to provide a spring and summer display.

The variety Mrs Iceton has smaller leaves that almost exceed the rainbow in their range of colour. It requires maximum light for best results. Much confusion exists over the proper naming of codiaeums and this plant is no exception, there being two other names to my knowledge – Annie Bier and Volcano. When it is seen almost erupting into colour, one realises that the last-mentioned name is not inappropriate. A point in favour of Mrs Iceton, not shared by many codiaeums, is the way in which foliage that has almost completely reverted to green will regain its exotic colouring as soon as the drab days of winter are left behind.

Columneas

These and allied plants, such as aeschynanthuses (syn. trichosporums) are not too difficult despite their exotic flowers. Being naturally trailing in habit, they should be placed where growth will trail down and show the flowering bracts to better advantage when they appear. When older plants become untidy new ones may be started from cuttings rooted in moist peat in warm conditions; whole strands will root if laid on the surface of the peat.

Dieffenbachias

All of these may safely be described as delicate plants that will require a minimum temperature of not less than 65°F. (18°C.) both by day and night. In the greenhouse, some varieties attain a maximum height of about 5 ft., by which time they will have lost many of their lower leaves and will be producing young plants at soil level from the base of the parent stem.

When the plant is no longer attractive, the main stem can be cut back almost to soil level, and the top portion may be propagated as a very large cutting; but unless conditions are good, one should not be too optimistic about the results. The bare stem of the plant can be cut up into pieces about 4 in. in length, each with a node (or joint), and laid on their sides partly buried in fresh peat. By keeping the peat at about 65°F. (18°C.), it is surprising the way in which some of these tough old stumps will develop into new plants.

Dieffenbachia has the unusual common name of Dumb Cane, which it gets from the fact that speech becomes difficult for a day or two should one inadvertently get the sap on one's tongue. However, since

Opposite: Codiaeum Mrs Iceton, the leaves of which almost exceed the rainbow in their range of colours

Bold, dark green leaves make *Dieffenbachia amoena* an exciting plant – but it needs space in which to display its attractions

dieffenbachias smell so abominably when cut, such a contingency is most unlikely.

Since the introduction of *Dieffenbachia amoena* from America about seven years ago it has gained many admirers. The bold, dark green leaves require space in which to spread, so spacious surroundings are the answer. Water should be given with care, as excessive wet will result in the main stem splitting at the base and eventually rotting. *D. arvida exotica* has been with us about the same length of time as *D. amoena* and is, if anything, more popular. Being more compact and slower growing than the latter it is much better suited to average room conditions.

Foliage plants are becoming increasingly popular for use in planted bowls, and florists frequently include one or two exotic plants, such as *D. exotica*, in order to catch the eye of the would-be customer. As a result, one is often asked how such arrangements should be cared for – a problem indeed. I find, however, that it is invariably better to place the container in a room temperature that will suit the more delicate subjects. While the majority of easier plants will tolerate the higher temperatures it will be found that the delicate plant will quickly succumb in colder conditions. In respect of watering, one should always aim at the happy medium, at all costs avoiding overwatering as many of these bowls have no drainage, so a build-up of water in the bottom of the container is a possibility that ought to be avoided.

Dracaenas

Several species of dracaena are available, and the best known is probably *Dracaena terminalis*, a somewhat trying plant which is prone to brown leaf tips, as a result of root failure. A light position is preferred, and it is especially important that soft water should be given in preference to hard tap water. The stiff red leaves are much prized by the enthusiastic flower arranger, but to me it seems almost criminal to strip leaves off this aristocrat among plants for such a purpose.

At present *D. mayii* is in short supply, but it seems reasonable, nevertheless, to predict a bright future for this attractive plant with its narrow, tightly clustered red leaves. It is a fine example of an excellent foliage plant that has been around the greenhouses of parks' departments for many a long day, and has only recently excited the attention of the commercial grower. Although stocks are in short supply, the dedicated gardener, willing to sacrifice plants in the process, can quickly increase his plants by means of stem and root cuttings, and by young offsets taken from the base of the main stem. *D. mayii* is not the easiest of plants indoors, but, as dracaenas go, it is less troublesome than many of its relatives.

Dracaena sanderiana has grey and white narrow leaves on slender stems, and presents something of a problem in respect of culture. Excessively wet compost allied to low temperatures will almost certainly result in browning of the leaf tips. Although plants with single stems may appear unimpressive, I find that when planted in groups of a dozen or more they are indis-

62

Opposite, top: Hedera helix Adam grafted onto a fatshedera stem (right) has as a companion *Dracaena mayii*

Opposite: Dracaena godseffiana Florida Beauty, a variety which has leaves heavily spotted with cream, and *Dracaena mayii* (left)

The aristocratic *Dracaena terminalis* has beautiful leaves of red and dark green colouring. Like all dracaenas it needs special care to give of its best

pensable for display work. Should one own a number of these plants it will be found that a much more pleasing effect can be achieved by potting several together; three plants to a 5-in. pot is about right. Overgrown plants can be cut back and will develop new shoots from the old stem, as well as from soil level.

A dracaena of distinctive appearance is *D. godseffiana* Florida Beauty, a variety with oval leaves borne close together on low growing stems and heavily spotted with cream.

Ficuses

Besides the ordinary Rubber Plant, *Ficus elastica decora*, (see p. 44) there are many other ficus plants available, some easy to care for, others not so easy. At the extreme ends of the scale, in respect of size, there is the stately Fiddle-leaved Fig, *F. lyrata*, and the creeping *F. radicans variegata*, neither of which is easy to grow. Given ideal conditions, *F. lyrata* reaches tree-like proportions in time, and will tolerate quite severe pruning when established. To succeed with the variegated *radicans*, a propagating case or a damp mossed stake would appear to be essential, as plants quickly deteriorate in the dry atmosphere of the average room.

It is not always realised that the creeping fig, *F. pumila*, a charming green plant of easy culture, can be encouraged to climb if a mossed stake, or piece of cork bark, is provided for the aerial roots to cling to. It is essential that the support should be kept moist and equally important that the compost should not become saturated, so fill a scent spray with water and use this for damping the support.

Ficus elastica tricolor is an attractive plant, similar to the ordinary Rubber Plant, but with variegated leaves of pink, cream and green. When introduced a few years ago it was hailed as being a plant of good temperament, needing little more care than the green Rubber Plant. This has not proved so in practice, as browning of leaf margins is still a problem yet to be overcome, and usually associated with wet, cold conditions. It does, however, have the remarkable capacity for growing away clean and strong for a second time when the stems have been cut to stumps of little more than 3 or 4 in. in height. So, do not completely despair when plants lose their leaves and are no longer attractive – instead, try cutting them back. Cut-back plants will, of course, require only the bare minimum amount of water until such time as new leaves are produced.

Fittonias

Fittonia argyroneura and *F. verschaffeltii* have similar habits of growth, but are easily distinguishable, the first having silvered leaves and the latter, leaves which

Ficus radicans variegata, a creeping variety which can be trained on a strip of cork bark or a mossed stake. If the support is kept moist this attractive but rather temperamental plant will be easier to grow

64

Neoregelia carolinae tricolor, an attractive and thoroughly reliable plant. A peculiarity is that the 'urn' which forms the centre of the plant must be kept full of water

Right: Neoregelia carolinae, showing the small mauve flowers in the centre of the 'urn'

Opposite: When grouping house plants, form is as important as colour. Note the contrasting shapes in the collection which gives heightened interest and pleasure

Right: The inflorescence of *Monstera deliciosa borsigiana* which, short-lived in itself, develops into an edible fruit with an unusual pineapple-banana flavour

Peperomia caperata, the curious flowers of which look like shepherds' crooks embedded among the crinkly leaves

are reddish-brown in colour. Both are suitable bottle garden plants and should be given a minimum temperature of at least 65°F. (18°C.) and a certain amount of humidity. Water is given in moderation; indeed, *F. argyroneura* has quite astonishing powers of recovery after the compost has become really bone-dry. Leaves suffering from drought will collapse to the point when they will appear to be quite shrivelled and lifeless; yet, after watering, they soon become firm again.

Hibiscuses

These are excellent room plants that will greatly benefit from being exposed to the maximum amount of sunshine, though the temperature need only be moderate. The exotic flowers last for a day or two only, but as one dies there always seems to be another in bud promising pleasure on another day. Correct watering is important; the compost must not at any time be allowed to dry out during the summer months, as loss of flowering buds will be the inevitable result.

My plant of *Hibiscus rosa-sinensis* is about 4 ft. in height and is kept in check by annual pruning in the autumn when it is obvious that no further flowers can be expected until the following spring. The variegated form, *H. rosa-sinensis cooperi*, has red flowers that appear infrequently. The graceful habit and light colouring

Flowers of *Hoya carnosa* a choice greenhouse or conservatory plant which provides a challenge to the house plant enthusiast

suggests, however, that it may well be a promising plant for the future. A cool, light place is most suitable, as plants will lose much of their bright colouring if temperatures are high and light is restricted.

Hoyas

Much prized for its exquisite, pendant clusters of flowers, *Hoya carnosa* is, nevertheless, not an easy plant to flower indoors. It is best planted out in the greenhouse, or conservatory, with the growth trained to overhead wires. The flowers will then be better appreciated and will also be more plentiful.

Hoya carnosa variegata is even more reluctant to produce flowers when its roots are confined to a pot, but the attractive foliage more than compensates for lack of flowers. Some of these have better coloured foliage than others, and it may well be worth while looking through your supplier's stocks in order to locate those with a pink flush of colouring. In common with all climbing plants, hoyas will benefit if supports can be provided for growth to twine around.

Isolepis gracilis (syn. Scripus cernuus)

As will be seen from the illustration of the lady with the hollow head (left), this is an adaptable plant. Trouble free, it puts up with wide variations in temperature, and asks for little more than sufficient water to keep the soil moist, and occasional feeding with liquid fertiliser. It is easily propagated by dividing the roots and potting them up individually in any reasonable

A miniature bulrush (*Isolepis gracilis*) put to unconventional use

Opposite: Peperomia sandersii

65

compost. Although it would appear to be a member of the grass family, it is in fact a miniature bulrush.

Maranta picturata

Maranta picturata is a difficult plant to grow, and not easy to obtain, but it is a particular favourite of mine and I hope that it will become more freely available later – hence my reason for including it. The leaves are light grey, compactly arranged with dark green margins and maroon undersides, and they seldom fail to attract attention. A shaded position, with a temperature of 65°F. (18°C.) and high humidity, will provide ideal growing conditions. Plants are increased by means of cuttings, which are prepared from pieces of growth about 4 in. in length with two or three leaves attached. Insert them in 3-in. pots of moist peat. They may also be increased by division in the early part of the year and, if one is lucky enough, plants will occasionally have a colony of self-set seedlings around them. However, it must be confessed that a heated greenhouse, with plants standing on a moist peat bed, is almost essential for the latter to take place. As a general guide, if delicate plants require a growing temperature of about 65°F. (around 18°C.) one may safely assume that at least 5°F. (3°C.) more heat will be needed when propagating new plants.

Persea gratissima (The Avocado Pear)

You buy the pear, plant the stone, and in time you will have the satisfaction of saying that you did it all yourself. Unfortunately, these plants grow rapidly indoors and the larger leaves tend to droop eventually. To keep the plant reasonably compact the leading shoots should be pinched out occasionally. In average room conditions the Avocado Pear will soon outgrow its allotted space, and the owner is then faced with the problem of what is to be done with it – few of us have the heart to put a healthy plant in the dust-bin. Sad to say, I cannot help here, as it often requires a little diplomacy and a chat with the local garage proprietor who may be prepared to accept it for his showroom. At all costs, keep away from your florist and nurseryman, as they have, no doubt, had to say 'No' in the past when asked to provide a home for overgrown Avocado Pears.

Planting is simple; a 5-in. pot filled with John Innes No. 2 Potting Compost and a pear stone planted with

Opposite: **An Avocado Pear grown from the stone – fun for adult and child alike**

Maranta picturata, **a choice plant with light grey leaves, margined with dark green and with maroon undersides**

the pointed end uppermost will soon develop roots if kept moist in a warm room.

Philodendron melanochrysum

The heart-shaped leaves with brown velvet colouring make this plant well worth trying, even though it has the reputation of being difficult. A temperature in the region of 65°F. (18°C.) and humid conditions are important considerations.

It is probably an ambitious thought for the indoor plantsman, but hanging baskets filled with these philodendrons can look a picture, and might be worth trying. I well remember the mystified observers in Paris a few years ago, at an international flower show which I attended, when they saw a fine basketful of *Philodendron melanochrysum* twist first one way then the other with no visible means of support, or propulsion. They were not to know that nylon fishing line supported the basket, and the circulating warm air in the building was keeping it on the move. It is odd that, at flower shows, the slightest movement, be it only a drip of water in a pool, will attract more attention than any of the exotic plant life in the vicinity!

Platycerium alcicorne

One of my favourite house plants, the Stag's Horn Fern, as it is called, is much less difficult indoors than its appearance at first sight suggests.

As the platyceriums are epiphytes, better results will be achieved if plants are attached to a piece of bark, or absorbent timber; or they can be planted in an old log or tree stump. The method employed is the same as that described for cryptanthus (see p. 35). Once established on their anchorage, platyceriums can remain there literally until they grow themselves out of house room. As some indication of their potential, I once measured a plant that was 6 ft. in length and the same across. The hanging basket in which it had been originally planted had long since disappeared in the heart of the plant.

The spectacular adult foliage of *Philodendron melanochrysum*, sometimes known as *Philodendron andreanum* at this stage of its life

Left: The Stag's Horn Fern, *Platycerium alcicorne*

Opposite: Scindapsus aureus, which can be grown on a support or as a trailing plant

When attached to bark it is usual for Stag's Horn Ferns to be hung on the wall so that their antler appearance can be set off to full advantage. There is an obvious precaution, however; the wall must be made of brick, or some other material that will not be harmed by moisture.

Watering is simply done by plunging both plant and anchorage in a bucket of water and allowing the surplus water to drain away before putting it back in position. A little liquid fertiliser mixed into the water will be beneficial, care being taken that the fertiliser is only of such strength that it changes the water to a light straw colour.

Scindapsuses

Scindapsus aureus is an attractive plant that will respond to the treatment generally recommended for philodendrons. With leaves of similar shape and shorter internodes than its parent, the variety Marble Queen lives up to its name for it has white marbled foliage. It is not an easy plant, the leaves being prone to browning at the edges when the plants are young and the roots weak. Once the plants have established themselves they are not so troublesome. When grown as an upright plant it is most essential that a moist support be used into which the plant can work its roots. If one is filling a container with exotic plants it is by far the most exciting choice for trailing over the edge.

Sparmannia africana

Sparmannia africana has two common names, the Indoor Lime, which it gets from the appearance of the cool, green foliage, and the African Wind Flower, because of the way in which the flowers open outwards at the slightest breath of wind.

In ideal conditions it will quickly outgrow its welcome, but one can quite severely prune the branches to shape at almost any time. It is not often grown commercially, as demand is very limited, and growth in greenhouse conditions is frequently rampant enough to become an embarrassment to the commercial grower. A fine plant for a cool, light room, it will give little trouble if regular feeding and annual potting on are not neglected. In common with many of the easier plants, it can be increased readily from cuttings, so it is advisable to start fresh plants every second or third year.

Tolmiea menziesii

Described as a hardy perennial herb, *Tolmiea menziesii* is also a fine indoor plant that is very much neglected

Sparmannia africana a fine plant for a cool, light room

in this respect. Outdoors the foliage will die back in winter, indoors it will remain evergreen.

This is a particularly easy plant to care for, and has the amusing common name of Pick-a-Back Plant, which it gets from the way young plantlets are formed and carried 'on the back' of older leaves. These young plantlets root with ease in ordinary compost if they are inserted with the parent leaf still attached. It was my four-year-old daughter's first introduction to the mysteries of propagation; she now seems to have developed a sort of obsession for nipping off these young plants and dibbing them into any pot of soil that is handy – consequently we have Pick-a-Backs sprouting everywhere!

I was surprised recently, when shown a sick tolmiea, to discover that it was infested with red spider mites, so keep a watchful eye for them. The leaves of tolmiea are green in colour and slightly crinkled, and form into neat hummocks over the pot, though they will in time hang down for some length.

PALMS

The taller palms of the kentia type revive memories of bygone days as far as indoor plants are concerned, though there does appear to be renewed interest in them. Tough as can be, the majority demand little more than a good compost, well-firmed in the pot, and an ample supply of moisture at the roots. The need for potting on is made obvious when the accumulated roots in the bottom of the pot begin to push the root ball out of the container.

Two small palms that seldom grow to more than 30in. in height are *Neanthe bella* and *Cocos weddeliana*; both are ideal for the bottle or dish garden indoors.

Tolmiea menziesii, the Pick-a-Back Plant

Below: A mature specimen of *Neanthe bella,* which is excellent when young for bottle or dish garden cultivation

FERNS

Though we are often informed that these went out of favour as room plants some years ago, there are still a surprisingly large number of ferns being grown. Pot-grown ferns abhor direct sunlight, and should have warm, moist conditions in which to grow. In a hot, dry atmosphere, particularly where gas may be present, the tips of fronds will quickly show their resentment by turning brown. Plant pots should be plunged to their rims in damp peat or sphagnum moss, and the foliage will benefit from regular spraying over with tepid water. Established plants will also improve if fed while actively growing. Many of the smaller ferns (*Pellaea rotundifolia, Pteris argyraea, P. cretica,* and *P. ensiformis victoriae* to name but a few) are excellent plants for use in bottle gardens.

There are few green-foliaged plants that can compare with the cool beauty of a well-grown plant of *Asplenium nidus,* the Bird's Nest Fern. It is seen to best effect when growing in a 5-in. or larger pot, and its appearance is enhanced when it is placed in the shade of bolder plants, such as the monstera. A temperature in the 60-65°F. (16-18°C.) range will suit it and, contrary to general advice, feeding with weak liquid fertiliser will preserve the pale green colouring of its leaves. When dark brown 'spider's legs' of roots begin to creep over the edge of the pot, it is an indication that potting on is necessary. Use a potting compost that contains lots of peat, leaf-mould and a little fresh sphagnum moss.

Should the leaves require cleaning, this must be done with a soft sponge and clear water, as they are very easily damaged. Oil-based cleaners will give the leaves a transparent appearance that will in time cause them to rot, so they should not be used.

Opposite: Pellaea rotundifolia, a small fern for bottle gardens and other forms of decoration

A delightful small fern, *Pteris ensiformis victoriae,* with variegated foliage

Ficus lyrata, the Fiddle-leaved Fig, a plant of great character and stately appearance

Chapter 6
Architectural Plants

Such a grand-sounding heading for a chapter as Architectural Plants conjures up thoughts of towering office blocks and vast carpeted foyers where all conversations are carried out in a discreet whisper – with a take-over bid in every brief case. Certainly the term 'architectural plant' does suggest one of fairly substantial proportions, and they are, in most cases, set off to better advantage in more spacious surroundings. This need not imply, however, that they have no place in the home, as most of these plants are, in fact, sold in a variety of pot sizes. Indeed, homes with larger rooms and entrance halls do accommodate many of these larger plants, though sometimes to the exclusion of a piece of furniture.

The available range of specimen indoor plants, be they architectural or otherwise, is limited to comparatively few species and varieties. No doubt many more plants could be listed as having architectural merit, but this seems quite pointless knowing that they are almost unobtainable commercially. Only very few of the commercial house plant growers are prepared to tie up capital in a long-term investment in specimen indoor plants, many of which take several years to mature. Because of their slow rate of development these plants are almost invariably costly purchases.

On the question of cost, the individual specimen plant may be expensive, but in the proper setting it is much more impressive than a nondescript collection of smaller plants, and in the end need not be so much more costly than a selection of small plants. Also, a larger plant will be much easier to care for than a collection of smaller ones, which dry out quite rapidly in warm conditions

SELECTING AND POSITIONING THE PLANTS

When selecting and positioning such plants, be it in the office or private house, allowance must be made for their suitability. In respect of height, there should be a minimum of 2 to 3 ft. of head room so that the plant has an opportunity to develop. Where spotlights are used to highlight aspects of interior décor, or the plants themselves, care must be taken to ensure that the plant is at least 4 ft. away from the light bulb or reflector. If there is a continual flow of people past the plant or plants, then they should be placed well away from their general route. This is to protect them from being damaged by passers-by brushing against them, and to deter inquisitive fingers from handling the leaves in an effort to decide whether they are real or plastic!

Although architects are very capable people where building design is concerned, many of them are lamentably ill-informed in respect of plants and their requirements. Elsewhere I have discussed the general requirements of indoor plants and their positioning (see pp. 16

75

to 21) and I have no wish to repeat my remarks here, except on one point, namely, the question of plant height in relation to the size of the pot in which the plant will be growing. When visualising a bold plant of some 8 to 10 ft. in height or with a wide spread, there is no point in providing a match-box-sized container in which to house the pot, as so often is the case. For larger plants the absolute minimum size of container is one with a diameter of 12 in. and a depth of not less than 10 in.

One further point on containers; I feel that they should be portable when housing larger plants. This will save a good deal of perspiration if it is decided to reposition the plant. Boxes, or containers, mounted on Easy-Glide castors will simplify matters to the point whereby a rearrangement of the plants can become a matter of course. Also, it makes life much easier for whoever has to do the cleaning when boxes can be moved around.

AROIDS

The *Araceae* and *Moraceae* (p. 26 and 44) are the families which provide the majority of plants that can be defined as architectural, mainly on account of their larger leaves and more stately appearance. The aroids

Pandanus veitchii, **a striking variegated-leaved plant. The leaves have saw-edged margins**
Opposite: **The bold plant in the foreground is** *Philodendron bipinnatifidum,* **its companion is** *Hedera canariensis,* **the Canary Island Ivy**

(*Araceae*), as well as including many of our bolder plants, also give us some of the most beautiful and delicate-foliaged hot greenhouse plants. Perhaps the most important aroid for this chapter is the well-known *Monstera deliciosa borsigiana* (see p. 26), sometimes wrongly referred to as *Philodendron pertusum*. (The latter is, in fact, a plant with smaller leaves and a more erect habit of growth.) Of all the many beautiful green-leaved plants in cultivation, Mother Nature surely excelled herself when devising the serrated, and eventually perforated, monstera leaf. Positioned where space is ample and temperature adequate the monstera will give lasting service with comparatively little attention.

Another aroid of spreading habit, with green finger-like leaves is *Philodendron bipinnatifidum* (see p. 28). Mention has been made elsewhere of the semi-retired gardener at our local railway station, and his devotion to, and ability with, plants. Perhaps the *P. bipinnatifidum* in the parcel office was his most spectacular plant, and much of the success was due to the aerial roots being allowed to drink up as much water as they required, instead of, as so often happens, being allowed to hang limply in a dry atmosphere. This was made possible by placing the plant pot in one end of a zinc trough and encouraging aerial roots, as they developed, to have a free run in the moist gravel in the bottom of the trough. This, by the way, is an excellent method of encouraging aroids to produce really bold leaves: stand them on the edge of a pool or water tank and give the aerial roots free run in the water. By so doing it will be found that the actual compost in the pot requires only the bare minimum of water.

Other philodendrons I mention only briefly on

Bold lines, as exemplified by these two plants, *Dracaena sanderiana* **(left) and** *Platycerium alcicorne* **are effective in simple room settings**

account of their scarcity. *Philodendron wendlandii* is a compact green plant with a shuttle-cock arrangement of the leaves that radiate from a low central crown; and Burgundy is an excellent and tolerant variety which will, in time, produce remarkably rich-coloured leaves, as much as 2 ft. in length and in no way belying its name. This latter plant will benefit considerably if its supporting stake has a thick wad of sphagnum moss bound to it with florist's wire; keep the moss moist and aerial roots will quickly begin to work their way into the damp material. Similar in appearance to Burgundy but with plain green leaves, *P. hastatum* (see p. 28) will also benefit from having its stake mossed; and, for the best results, the temperature should not be allowed to drop below 65°F. (18°C.).

ORNAMENTAL FIGS

The *Moraceae,* or Fig Family, provide us with an incredible range of ficus or Rubber Plants; from the creeping or climbing (if placed against a damp wall in the greenhouse) *Ficus pumila* to the majestic *F. lyrata* (see p. 64). In the architectural group I have not included the upright *F. elastica decora*. Instead, one should endeavour to grow something rather more spectacular by acquiring one of these Rubber Plants when it has formed itself into a natural tree shape. This they do without help on reaching a height of about 8 ft., or when the growing tip has been deliberately cut out. Planted out into beds filled with good potting compost these plants will grow at a remarkable pace, putting on as many as 50 new leaves on a single branch in the course of one growing season.

Ficus lyrata, (see p. 64) commonly named the Fiddle-leaved Fig because of its fiddle-shaped leaves, develops a sizeable trunk when at home in its surroundings. When well settled in and growing away it will tolerate quite severe pruning, though dark conditions and inadequate temperature will quickly result in the loss of the lower leaves, and pruning will be more of a dream than a reality.

A ficus of quite different appearance, having nothing of the stiff habit of its relatives, is the elegant Weeping

Where space is available, *Phoenix roebelenii* a graceful palm, is well worth considering

signs that they are returning to favour. Many of them make excellent indoor or office plants, and in a larger area well-grown plants of *Kentia belmoreana* or *Phoenix roebelenii* are well able to hold their own with more recent introductions. The lasting qualities of kentia are almost legendary; the phoenix is a little more difficult. Both require copious watering in the summer months, and regular potting on is essential, otherwise the mass of accumulated roots will begin to push the plant and compost upwards and almost out of the pot in time.

PANDANUSES

The vicious saw-edged leaf of the pandanus (the species *veitchii* is probably the best) make it essential that this plant should be positioned where passers-by will not come in contact with the leaves. Failure to do so frequently results in costly replacement of laddered nylons! This is generally an easy plant to grow, and ideal for brightening up the plant display that is tending to become too green. To preserve the variegated colouring a light position is essential, and water should be given when the soil is seen to be dry and not as a daily ritual.

DRACAENAS

For that exotic Palm Beach effect, few plants can compete with the dracaenas (unless it is a palm, of course), and in particular *Dracaena marginata*, a comparatively recent introduction to the house plant

Above: **The climbing or trailing *Ficus pumila* grown here on a piece of cork bark**

***Kentia belmoreana,* a palm with almost legendary lasting qualities**

Fig, *F. benjamina*. This is often rather a perplexing plant when first put in position, as it seems almost inevitable that it will have some yellow leaves until it settles down. These should be removed, if only to improve the plant's appearance, and it will be found that in most cases the plant will establish itself in a week or two.

Ficus plants in general should be inspected regularly when grown in pots standing on moist gravel or peat, as they are notorious for rooting through the holes in the bottom of the pot. This is one reason why it is often better to plant ficuses in boxes of compost where they can have a free root run, and grow much more rapidly and strongly as a result.

A SPECIAL FAVOURITE

One of my particular favourites in the architectural range of house plants, brings back fond memories of an old New Zealand friend, Mr Andrew Anderson. Many years ago he introduced the plant to me by writing the name *Brassaia actinophylla* on a greenhouse door and saying, with a finger stabbing at the name, 'This is a plant you must grow if you want specimen plants'. The plant, sold here as *Schefflera actinophylla,* deserves to be much more popular than it is, for it is a mixture of boldness and elegance; even a 15-ft. specimen does not appear in any way heavy.

PALMS

Palms, like aspidistras, conjure up thoughts of Victoriana, and are not so popular to-day, though there are

range. It is a fairly easy 'doer', that, in common with most dracaenas, sheds its lower leaves as it increases in height. Far from being detrimental, this process often gives the plant a more elegant appearance, with its dull red-margined leaves spiking out in all directions.

Two more dracaenas that are somewhat more temperamental, so not for the novice, are *D. deremensis* and *D. massangeana*. The former, which has grey-green striped leaves, must have a minimum temperature of 65°F. (18°C.). Watering must also be done with great care; it must never be too wet or the leaves will brown at the tips and edges. *D. massangeana*, which will also test the grower's skill, has strap-like leaves, margined green with mustard-coloured centres. It is probably a more attractive plant when it has reached a height of 4 to 5ft., and certainly it is better if given sufficient space for the leaves to spread naturally.

Left: *Dracaena massangeana* (left), *Sansevieria trifasciata laurentii* (centre) and *Platycerium alcicorne* (right)

Fatsia japonica* and the graceful, variegated *Hibiscus rosa-sinensis cooperi

Right: The bold pink bract and the handsome leaves of *Aechmea rhodocyanea* make this a striking house plant. It can be grown without difficulty if a minimum temperature of 60°F. (16°C.) is maintained

Begonias, a trailing ivy, cyciamen, *Philodendron melanochrysum* and an Avocado Pear form an interesting group. With such variety in the plant material a plain background will offset the plants to advantage

Citrus mitis, the Calamondin Orange, a plant which needs the maximum amount of sunshine available if it is to flower and fruit well

Left: Caladium Mary Moir, an especially attractive variety of a beautiful foliage plant. The leaves have an almost transparent appearance, and, as can be seen, are delicately marked

Opposite, below: Dracaena marginata, with dull red-margined leaves, is excellent for display as a specimen plant

The fast-growing Australian Wattle or Silk Oak, *Grevillea robusta*

Right: Aralia elegantissima, an elegant foliage plant, with *Pandanus veitchii* in the foreground

TETRASTIGMA VOINIERIANUM

Lastly, the tetrastigmas, and in particular the species *Tetrastigma voinierianum,* which excites the interest of those who prefer their plants to have interestingly shaped foliage. Certainly it has an advantage over most other large plants in that it is quick growing. In ideal greenhouse conditions 'rampant' is probably a better word, as tetrastigmas are difficult to keep in check once they have decided to become entangled with their neighbours. As with ficuses, they too present difficulties when their roots decide to go in search of something other than that which is available in their pots. Growth is kept in check by frequently winding it back and forth around itself; string is unnecessary, as self-clinging tendrils quickly attach themselves to everything and anything. The compost should be kept moist and frequent feeding is essential. However, guard against excessive wet which results in leaves – and, in extreme cases, actual growing shoots – being shed.

81

Left: The elegant Weeping Fig, *Ficus benjamina,* and *Dracaena deremensis,* an attractive but somewhat temperamental plant

Below left: Dracaena sanderiana, one of the author's favourite house plants. It has grey and white narrow leaves

Below: Neanthe bella and the trailing *Hedera* Little Diamond

Opposite: Sansevieria trifasciata laurentii, a first-class architectural plant, and *Begonia masoniana* in the foreground

A well-planted bottle garden which includes plants of *Ficus radicans variegata, Scindapsus aureus* Marble Queen, *Peperomia magnoliae-folia, Maranta leuconeura kerchoveana* and *Cocos weddeliana*

Chapter 7
Bottle Gardens

Bottle gardens are adaptions of the Wardian case principle of keeping tender, moisture-loving plants in an environment that would otherwise be difficult to simulate in the average living room. Dr Ward, after whom Wardian cases are named, was a keen plants-man who discovered that tender ferns lived for many years, virtually without attention, in the atmosphere of his ingenious cases, which were first used in about 1830.

When cases are hermetically sealed, watering is unnecessary, as moisture transpiring from the plants' leaves condenses on the inside of the glass container, and eventually finds its way back into the soil. Completely sealed containers are, however, less attractive than those with a small opening because the film of moisture which forms on the inside of the glass obscures the plants from view. Bottle gardens with open tops will require a little water very occasionally, when the plants are seen to be flagging, or when the soil surface is obviously dry. Watering should be done by trickling the water gently on to the soil surface by means of a flexible rubber hose pipe (the one from the washing machine is ideal).

Disused carboys make excellent bottle gardens, as they are spacious inside and permit the use of slightly taller plants, though sweet bottles and clear glass jars of various kinds may also be used for smaller, or even individual, plants. Almost the first step on acquiring a carboy will be the need to give it a thorough cleaning with detergent, both inside and out, in order to remove stains and any harmful residue. Be warned, however, that the use of hot water is positively not advised, because of the risk of cracking the glass.

THE PLANTING OPERATION

Before planting begins the following materials should be at hand: sufficient pebbles ($\frac{3}{8}$-in. ballast, from your local builders' merchant, is ideal) to provide a 2-in. layer in the bottom of the bottle (these should be thoroughly wetted before putting in position); a small amount of charcoal (from any gardening shop) for mixing with the compost (see below) to prevent it becoming sour too quickly. Sour soil inevitably results in the formation of an unsightly coating of algae on the surface of the compost. Large carboys will need about a 5-in. layer of compost, which should be of an open texture. John Innes No. 2 Potting Compost would be a suitable medium with the addition of two handfuls of sharp grit to improve drainage.

Use a funnel, shaped from a piece of cardboard, to pour the materials through the narrow neck of the bottle and into the desired position.

PLANTS TO CHOOSE

Next, and most important, is the choice of plants. Here

85

it must be emphasised that only slow-growing plants should be used (a suggested list of plants that are reasonably easy to purchase will be found on p. 88). A florist friend informs me that his charge for dismantling overgrown carboys is more than his charge for arranging plants initially – so beware. The same friend illustrated his point when he showed me a carboy that had been planted up less than one year previously with the apparently harmless Dead Nettle, *Gynura sarmentosa*. In a matter of months the plant had filled all the available space in the carboy and had a few shoots inspecting the prospects outside the bottle!

PLANTS TO AVOID

The use of flowering plants presents problems, for when flowers fade and die they become vulnerable to one or other of the fungus diseases, which will quickly spread to other plants in the container if left unchecked. Having warned against the use of flowering plants, I can see in my mind's eye an established bottle garden in perfect condition, in the centre of which nestled an African Violet in full flower and obviously not in the least concerned about having been an 'intruder' for the previous two years. In general, however, though you may be tempted to experiment, it is better to concentrate on foliage plants when making your selection.

Purchased plants ought to be in pots no larger than 3 in. in diameter if they are to conveniently pass through the neck of the bottle. Plants in larger pots, besides being too tall or spreading in themselves, suffer considerably from having their roots mutilated in the planting process. Also, care must be taken to choose plants with flexible leaves that will bend easily as they are lowered into the bottle.

SIMPLE TOOLS AS PLANTING AND CULTURAL AIDS

Some simple tools will be needed for planting, pruning and cleaning. Mine are nothing more than a few 2-ft. canes, to the ends of which I tie a teaspoon (as substitute for a trowel), a table fork (for a rake), and an old

Making a bottle garden. The compost is funnelled into position through a roll of stiff paper. Any contours that are desired can be made at this stage by mounding up the soil

The first plant is carefully lowered into the bottle and is then moved to the desired position using a long-handled tool

cotton reel wedged onto the end of a cane, which is used for firming the soil around the roots after planting. For pruning, my favourite tool is a razor blade secured into a cleft in the end of a cane. For a scavenging tool I follow in the steps of the park keeper and tie a nail to the end of a cane; this is used for spearing yellow leaves and severed pieces that the pruner has dealt with.

A TRIAL RUN

To obviate the need for difficult manoeuvring of plants in the confined space of the container it is better to do a mock-up outside the bottle first, in order to achieve the desired effect. Do this by preparing a bed of compost of approximately the same dimensions as the surface area of the soil in the container, and on this arrange the plants to your satisfaction; it is then an easy matter to

An elegant Wardian case – the forerunner of the modern bottle garden – which first came into use about 1830. In these containers, tender, moisture-loving plants can be grown to perfection with very little attention

A slight depression is made for the plant's roots and the compost is then firmed around the plant with a home-made rammer made by fixing a cotton reel to a bamboo cane

Planting almost completed. With a little practice it will be found that the rammer can be used with considerable dexterity

87

place them accordingly in the bottle. The standard car-boy will accommodate five or six small plants; if more than this number are planted they will quickly become congested.

MANOEUVRING PLANTS INTO POSITION

Most care will be needed when the actual planting operation takes place. Although it may appear harsh, I find that using my park keeper's prodder to spear through the root ball is the simplest way of inserting plants and manoeuvring them into position. One of the other tools can then be used to hold the plant firm while the prodder is withdrawn. I often feel that the dextrous use of elongated chop-sticks would be the perfect answer to planting. Or, as an acquaintance once suggested, bottle gardens should be fitted with zip fasteners! Dr Ward would seem to have had the ideal

Three dracaenas growing with *Begonia rex* and an ivy in a bowl of pleasing outline

answer when he fitted a door in the side of his more ornamental Wardian cases (see p. 87).

In common with the majority of foliage plants, your carboy will require a light position and protection from strong sunlight. Ornamentation in the way of stones, bark, twigs, wee men and such like is purely a matter of personal taste. These can be used to good effect if they are placed with care and used sparingly.

BOTTLE GARDEN PLANTS

Acorus gramineus variegatus	Erect golden grass.
Adiantum cuneatum	The delicately-leaved Maidenhair Fern.
Asplenium nidus	Only for larger bottles, as eventually this plant becomes rather large.
Begonia boweri	This plant will pay for the bother of finding a supplier.
Begonia rex	Only the smaller-leaved sorts. There is a danger of mildew attacking the leaves of these plants in close, damp conditions.
Codiaeums (crotons)	Many of these develop into very substantial plants, often outgrowing the small greenhouse, let alone the bottle garden – so select with care.
Codiaeum pictum and *C.* Apple Leaf	Both *Codiaeum pictum* and the variety Apple Leaf will remain reasonably small, though their colouring, yellow and green, is rather dull when compared with that of most codiaeums.
Cryptanthuses	In many varieties – choose those with smaller leaves and more compact rosettes.
Dracaena godseffiana Florida Beauty	See description on p. 64.
Dracaena sanderiana	Becomes tall in time, but useful for providing a little height in the centre of the arrangement.
Ficus pumila	A quick grower, but regular pruning will keep it in check.
Fittonia verschaffeltii	See description on p. 64.
Hederas (ivies)	Select the small-leaved, variegated ones and cut them back when they spread too far.
Hoya carnosa variegata	Easily checked by pruning if it becomes too invasive. Can either be used as a ground-cover plant or be tied to a short cane to give a little extra height.
Maranta leuconeura erythrophylla	A fine plant capable of being a feature if planted by itself in the bottle garden, with only the odd bit of ivy or *Ficus pumila* to act as a foil.
Maranta l. kerchoveana	Only for larger containers.
Peperomias	*Peperomia magnoliaefolia, P. hederaefolia* and *P. caperata.* The last two form large clumps that will be difficult to prune, so use them only in more spacious bottle gardens.
Pteris cretica	One of the many smaller ferns that are perfect for this purpose.
Sansevieria hahnii variegata	Expensive and scarce.
Sansevieria trifasciata laurentii	Not one of the best, but it offers a pleasing change of leaf shape.

Codiaeums, superb plants for providing spectacular foliage effects

Asplenium nidus, the lovely fresh-green Bird's Nest Fern

Caladium Mrs F. M. Joyner, another beautifully marked variety providing much pleasure

Begonia rex, one of the finest of all foliage plants, is available in many varieties

Opposite: A monstera of tree-like dimensions which is admirably suited to a corner position. The broad, deeply-cut leaves have a sympathetic foil in the modern sideboard

The tall Weeping Fig, *Ficus benjamina,* is in complete harmony with the leather chair and wooden panelling and shows the advantages of blending plants with natural materials

Chapter 8
Flowering House Plants

Rather than write a few brief words about the maximum number of plants, I have in this chapter on flowering house plants endeavoured to discuss some of the established favourites in more detail, and to include a selection of the plants that have become popular in recent years.

In general, the needs of flowering plants indoors are very similar to those of other plants, as described in Chapter 2, Routine Culture (p. 16). The way in which some plants are inclined to shed flowers, and sometimes buds, when introduced to room conditions often gives rise for some concern. Much of the flower drop that occurs can be attributed to buffeting in transit, and to the change in conditions in respect of light and temperature. More often than not it will be found that plants quickly settle down in their new environment, and that flower production indoors presents few problems. However, permanently saturated compost and dark corners will result in weak growth and flowers that will drop at a touch.

There is no doubt that the condition of a flowering plant when purchased can influence its future life in the home. Unless flowers are especially wanted to create a favourable initial impression, the plants should almost all be purchased at the earlier stage of growth – to be more specific, when they have some colour showing and an adequate supply of buds, formed and forming, to follow. There are a few exceptions, however, two of these being the pot chrysanthemum and the poinsettia. The latter should be well coloured and the chrysanthemum ought to have a good percentage of buds open, though not fully.

Anthuriums

Here we have further proof of the importance of the aroid family to the house plant grower. The large-flowered (or, more accurately, large-spathed) *Anthurium andreanum* requires a minimum temperature of 70°F. (21°C.) and a very humid atmosphere, so it is only suitable as a temporary room plant. It is also very costly.

The newly introduced variety, *A.* Guatamalan, is less demanding, needing a temperature of about 65°F. (18°C.) and less humidity. It is also more shapely, and the orange-red spathes are produced much more freely. (Though expensive, mature anthurium 'flowers' have a water life of five to seven weeks from the time of cutting.)

Smaller and more compact than the previous types, *A. scherzerianum,* is, understandably, better known by its common name of Flamingo Flower. This plant does well in a light though not too sunny window, and appreciates a thoroughly well-drained and open compost. Soft water, with the chill taken off it, is

Aphelandra Brockfeld (far left), *Beloperone guttata* (top right) and *Saintpaulia* Englert's Diana Pink

Opposite: Azalea indica, one of the most popular of all winter-flowering plants for the home from November onwards

Anthurium scherzerianum the aptly named Flamingo Flower, is, like the bird, a lover of warm conditions. This plant does well in a light but not too sunny window

preferred; and if at all possible, the room temperature should not drop below 60°F. (16°C.). Soil, as such, is not important, the main compost ingredients being peat, leaf-mould, fresh sphagnum moss and a little dried cow dung – the object being to prepare an open spongy mixture. Crock the pot, and add a few crocks to the potting mixture as well, to further assist drainage. To improve their appearance, the spathes should be supported by a thin cane or wire; if wire is used, make a loop at the top in which to rest the stem, placing the wire just below the coloured spathe.

Aphelandras

There is little to choose between *Aphelandra* Brockfeld and *A. squarrosa louisae*. The former has more attractive foliage and the leaves are stiffer and carried almost horizontal to the main stem. The latter is less attractive in respect of foliage, but produces several yellow bracts to each stem, whereas Brockfeld is more inclined to have a single bract.

Both varieties are, without doubt, among the most trying of indoor flowering plants to care for. Dry roots and starvation are the main causes of failure, and these need be neglected on only one occasion for irreparable damage to be done. Aphelandras fill their pots with roots in a remarkably short space of time, so, from the moment they are purchased, they need lots of water and lots of fertiliser (the manufacturer's recommended dilution can be exceeded for aphelandras and no harm will be done).

Azaleas

The pot-grown *Azalea indica* is one of our most attractive plants, and is available in many colours for about six months of the year, from November onwards. At no time must it be allowed to dry out, and frequent syringing of the foliage will help to create the moist atmosphere that is so important to its well being. It is one of the few plants that one can be quite specific about in respect of watering. When purchased, almost all of the larger plants are in effect miniature standard specimens, having a short woody stem between pot and foliage. The properly watered plant should have a dark water mark about half way up this stem; if there is no mark the plant is too dry, and if the mark is near where the branches begin it is too wet. It is as simple as that.

Dead flowers should be removed regularly, and when the flowers have finished the plant is placed in a cooler room where it will require less water. During May, when frosts are less likely, the plant should be plunged to its pot rim in a sunny position in the garden, or in an airy cold frame that can have its cover removed during the day. Keep the compost moist and feed with liquid fertiliser during the summer months, when the foliage should also be sprayed over regularly. Before frosts are likely the plant must be moved into a cool room; and when buds begin to form, warmer conditions will encourage their development. When the plant is in flower the temperature can again be reduced. The first year after purchase a plant might not flower so well, but once adjusted to the suggested routine it will

provide a remarkable annual show of colour.

Begonias (see p. 56)

Beloperone guttata

Much of the popularity of *Beloperone guttata* is due to the apt common name of Shrimp Plant, which it gets from the shrimp-like appearance of the dull orange-coloured bract (the flowers are inconspicuous). Although normally quite small, reaching a height of about 18 in. indoors, *Beloperone guttata* can be grown into a specimen plant in a comparatively short space of time. Some years ago, at the Paris Floralies, my eyes seemed to deceive me when I saw a Shrimp Plant of at least 5 ft. in height, with a diameter of at least 3 ft. and bracts almost 6 in. in length. Later I had the good fortune to meet an employee of the nursery responsible for growing this monster. Taking his advice, an experiment was carried out, and we grew plants from

a height of 12 in. (in 5-in. pots) in the May of one year to over 4 ft. (in 8-in. pots) by May of the following year. Regular feeding and potting on was the answer, plus the fact that all bracts were removed as they appeared, so preventing the plant using up energy in their production. (A useful tip for many flowering plants – build up a plant before allowing it to bloom.) These plants were grown in a heated greenhouse, and would be an impossibility indoors, I imagine!

The feeding lesson can, however, still apply to the window-sill plant, but it would be better to feed in spring and summer when new leaves are being produced. When bracts lose their attractiveness they should be removed, and at the same time plants can be pruned to a better shape. Firm trimmings, about 3 in. in length, will not be difficult to root if placed around the edge of small pots filled with John Innes No. 1 Potting Compost.

A pot chrysanthemum at the right stage for
purchase. If bought at this stage, with most of
the buds just opening, the full flowering period
of the plant – at least six weeks – can be enjoyed

Opposite: A distinctive cyclamen – Silver Leaf.
The leaves are margined with silver giving it a
more attractive appearance than the typical
florists' cyclamen

Chrysanthemums

By using artificial light to extend winter day length, or
by covering the plants with black polythene in summer
to shorten the day, the nurseryman is able to offer pot-
grown chrysanthemums on any day of the year. Also,
by incorporating growth-depressant chemicals in the
potting mixture, the height of the plant can be restricted to between 15 and 20 in. Such plants should be
purchased when showing a reasonable amount of
colour and never when in tight bud. A good-quality
plant in a 5-in. pot will have about 20 flowers and can
almost be guaranteed to last for a full six weeks indoors.
After flowering, they can be planted out in the garden,
but, no longer being influenced by the chemical

restriction on growth, the plant will attain the height
of a normal garden chrysanthemum. Indeed, if planted
out in time for the plants to develop a reasonable length
of stem, it is possible for them to flower in their pots in
the early part of the year, and for the same plants to
flower later in the garden.

Columneas (see p. 60)

Cyclamen

Almost all plants grown commercially are raised from
seed and may take anything from 12 to 18 months
before producing enough flowers to be considered
saleable. During the major part of this time the plants
are kept at a temperature in the region of 55°F. (13°C.)

and ventilators are opened on every favourable occasion, so providing cool, airy conditions for most of the time. (For seed germination the temperature is in the region of 70°F. [21°C.].)

Having spent its entire life in light and airy surroundings, it is not surprising that a cyclamen plant quickly reacts against hot, dry room conditions by producing sickly yellow leaves and drooping flowers. A cool, light room provides ideal surroundings. Watering should be done thoroughly, allowing the compost to dry out (but never to become bone-dry) before watering again. The corm will not be damaged by water, but care must be taken not to get water in amongst the flower and leaf stalks, as they will be inclined to rot.

A neighbour, who could keep a cyclamen in perfect health for anything up to five months, always swore by, and performed, a weekly ritual that she remembered reading of some years before. It meant having a bowl of about 12 in. in diameter, in the centre of which she placed a block of wood about 1½ in. in thickness. Water was then poured into the bowl so that it did not quite cover the surface of the block when this was held down in the centre of the bowl. The cyclamen pot was then placed on the wood, which remained permanently moist. Each Saturday morning the moment of the week arrived when boiling water was poured from a kettle onto the block of wood – enough to replace the amount of water lost to the atmosphere during the week. When required, the compost in the pot was watered in the usual way. Though the purist may frown – and I

A Hortensia hydrangea. There are numerous varieties in shades of pink, rose, red and white

Below: the attractive *Hypocyrta glabra,* a comparatively new addition to the present range of house plants, has orange flowers and glossy, dark green foliage

cannot decide whether to approve or not – the cyclamen obviously liked this treatment.

For every success there must surely be a score of failures when attempting to keep cyclamen corms from one year to the next. It does seem, however, that once a corm has been successfully treated in this way it can be kept for a number of years without too much bother. Under normal conditions, the plant so treated is seldom as good as those grown from seed in the greenhouse. Nevertheless, there is a sense of satisfaction when success is achieved, so the following advice is offered. When the flowers have finished and the leaves begin to yellow and fall, water should be gradually reduced until the soil is quite dry. For preference the corm is left in its pot, which is placed on its side under the staging in a greenhouse. If a greenhouse is not available, a cool room or sheltered corner outside is the next best thing. In May, the plant should be knocked out of its pot and some of the old soil carefully removed and replaced with John Innes No. 2 Potting Compost. The plant can be left outside until mid-September when it is gradually introduced to warmer conditions (too sudden a change of temperature can be damaging). When the plants are established, they should be fed with liquid fertiliser.

Hibiscus (see p. 65)

Hoyas (see p. 65)

Hydrangeas

The hydrangeas are ideal dual-purpose plants, obtainable in shades of pink, red, white and blue, though the blue colours are in fact pink varieties that have been induced to change colour by adding carefully controlled quantities of alum to the potting soil. Never allow them to dry out, feed them well and they will be little trouble if given a light position. When they have finished flowering indoors they can be planted out in the garden – hence the dual-purpose reference.

Hypocyrtas

This is a comparatively new introduction and makes an interesting addition to the range of flowering house plants. It is commonly named the Clog Plant on account of the attractive orange-coloured flowers that resemble a miniature clog. Even when not in flower the mass of glossy, dark green leaves are an attraction in themselves, and, provided it receives the standard treatment for indoor plants, it is not difficult to care for. Growth may be trimmed into shape at almost any time after flowering and if used as 3-in. long cuttings, the healthy trimmings will root readily if one or two of the lower leaves are removed before inserting. It is an excellent choice for growing in a container or basket suspended from the ceiling near a light window.

Impatiens

Ease of propagation has established the Busy Lizzies (*Impatiens sultanii*) as some of our most popular and homely flowering plants. They root quite quickly, either in a proper compost or placed in water, and it is interesting to grow them in a clear glass bottle so that roots can be observed as they begin to grow. For growing plants, a light sunny window is the place, and they should not be allowed to dry out, otherwise the flowers and buds will drop. They can be trimmed and reshaped at any time, and require regular feeding when in active growth if the leaves are to be kept healthy and green. If you want a plant as large as the one seen in the window down the road, pot your plant into a larger container using moist John Innes No. 2 Potting Compost.

The newer species *Impatiens petersiana,* with dull red leaves and scarlet flowers, will require more than the usual amount of fertiliser, and more frequent potting on. A watchful eye should be kept on this impatiens for red spider; leaves becoming brown and dry are signs of their presence.

Poinsettias

Poinsettias have green leaves and insignificant flowers that are surrounded by brightly-coloured bracts, which are actually coloured leaves. The red-coloured plant is best known, though there are equally good white, pink and cream-pink varieties available. The modern poinsettia is surely one of the most remarkable plants of recent years. It has now lost its too-delicate-for-words image and become an established favourite that is thoroughly reliable. A sweeping statement, maybe(I know there are still some that fail inexplicably), but the way in which the public and florist alike have accepted the new variety Paul Mikkelsen is abundant proof of its durability.

Although the greenhouse cultivation of this variety is in itself a fascinating subject, I will only very briefly comment on this aspect. New techniques and the use of growth-depressant chemicals are responsible for the compact plant, seldom more than 24 in. tall, that is today offered for sale. Intense red bracts are no longer confined to the pre-Christmas months of the year, as the nurseryman is able to use black polythene to restrict the amount of light available to the plant, so inducing it to flower at an unnatural time. As with chrysanthemums, poinsettia flower buds initiate when the day reaches a given length, and when grown naturally the poinsettia does so in about the third week of October. The light factor is probably the most important single reason why it is difficult to flower poinsettias indoors. In the home, they usually have the normal day length of light, and are then subjected to an additional five to six hours of artificial light in the evening, so plants continue to grow instead of developing flowers and bracts. The answer is to grow them in a room where they will only get natural daylight. A sunny window will be ideal and will only be too hot for them on the very brightest of days. A temperature of around 60°F. (16°C.) will be perfectly adequate.

A golden rule with watering is to water when necessary and not at set times, nor just for the sake of it. Feeding is not important once the bracts have formed; before this, apply weak liquid fertiliser regularly.

Reports indicate that it is possible to have plants in colour for eight months or more from the time of

Above: **Impatiens petersiana,** a species with dark red leaves and scarlet flowers

Below: A poinsettia. These plants are much in demand as their gay bracts, usually bright red but also now available in pink and white, are unusually decorative

purchase. This would, however, be the exception, and one would normally expect a flowering time of between six and eight weeks.

As the flowers in the centre of the bract begin to rot, or drop off, the bract itself will gradually begin to disintegrate. At about this time, the leaves will also begin to turn yellow and will fall at a touch. When the plant is no longer attractive the main stem should be cut back to a height of about 6 in. from the soil surface. The flow of sap from the cut stem will do no harm and can either be left to dry naturally, or it can be checked by applying powdered charcoal or moist sand to the wound.

A week or two before cutting the stem, water should be gradually reduced until the compost is almost dry. If not considered unsightly, the plant can remain in the window; failing this it should be stored in a warm place, as cold conditions will lessen its chance of survival. While it is resting, the compost must be kept almost dry until new growth appears, when normal watering can be gradually resumed. At this time the plant can be potted on, or re-potted in the same pot after first removing some of the old soil; John Innes No. 2 Potting Compost is the best to use. If the plant is successfully flowered for a second time one should not

expect indoor growth to produce quite such large bracts as those of greenhouse-grown plants.

Saintpaulias

African Violets, as saintpaulias are called, are among the most perplexing of all our indoor plants, and almost everyone seems to have attempted growing them at one time or other. Most people shake their heads in disbelief when they see a really well-flowered plant, saying they have tried saintpaulias unsuccessfully so many times. The natural follow-up question is, 'What is the secret?'

Mrs Murray, an old friend and true expert on the subject, attributes her success to a mysterious ingredient which she refers to as T.L.C. – tender, loving care. Though T.L.C. is important, there is a great deal more to it than that, as our expert well knows. To achieve success there are, to my mind, three essential factors that cannot be ignored: light, adequate temperature and proper watering.

According to most of the recognised experts, saintpaulias should have approximately 14 hours of light each day. So it is a question of the lightest possible window during the day, and supplementary artificial light in the evening. I have found that most of the

Saintpaulias (African Violets), so attractive when in full flower, need light, adequate temperature and proper watering to succeed. Shallow containers, such as those below, are especially well suited to their rounded profiles

Opposite, above: Aphelandra Brockfeld, a variety which usually bears single yellow bracts on each stem and has silver and green foliage

Opposite, below: Anthurium scherzerianum

Left: Aphelandra squarrosa louisae which usually produces several bracts on each stem. It requires moist, warm conditions for success

Opposite: Spathiphyllum Mauna Loa, a more recent introduction than *S. wallisii.* It is a bolder plant but requires similar cultural conditions; protection from direct sunlight, regular feeding and annual potting on in spring

The heavily-scented *Stephanotis floribunda.* A light position and reasonable temperature are the main requirements of this choice greenhouse plant which is now becoming popular as a house plant

greatly improved strains of saintpaulia now on sale will do perfectly well on a sunny window-ledge, needing protection from only the strongest mid-day sun. Have a care, though; sunshine on wet leaves will be damaging, so avoid wetting leaves when watering.

Often I have listened to the tale of woe as someone has described how wonderfully well their African Violet did in the steamy kitchen window during the summer, only to gradually succumb with the approach of winter. It is the common fault of inadequate temperature that is responsible for leaves becoming darker in colour and beginning to shrivel as cold conditions and fluctuating temperatures have their effect. Although plants will survive at lower temperatures, I have found that a minimum of 65°F. (18°C.) is essential if plants are to bear any resemblance to good health and produce fresh leaves at the same time.

Some time ago, on recommending the use of tepid water for saintpaulias, I was just a trifle nonplussed when a listener, in all seriousness, asked where it could be purchased! As hot water can be more harmful than cold, care should be taken to use water that has just got the chill off; I find that a container of water placed in a warm room overnight is ideal for use the following morning. Water must be kept off the leaves and away from the central crown of the plant, and is best given by placing the pot in a shallow saucer of water and allowing the plant to drink up all it requires before tipping away the surplus. Never allow plant pots to stand in water for any length of time.

Damaged leaves and dead flowers must be removed as soon as they are seen in order to prevent rot setting up in the centre of the plant. When cleaning plants in this way, it is important that the complete leaf or flower stalk should be removed, leaving no pieces that are likely to rot if left attached to the plant.

Cuttings present little difficulty if firm, clean leaves are inserted in a peat and sand mixture; endeavour to maintain a temperature in the region of 65°F. (18°C.). They will also form roots in water. When the young plants clustered around the parent leaf are large enough to handle, and have a reasonable amount of root attached, they should be gently teased apart. A number of individual little plantlets will result; handled carefully, these can be potted up individually, or spaced out in a seed box filled with a mixture of two-thirds John Innes No. 2 Potting Compost to one-third clean peat. (This mixture will be suitable for saintpaulias at all stages of growth.) Treated in this way, plants with single crowns will result and flowers will stand boldly away from the overlapping rosette of neat leaves. If left undivided, flowers and leaves intermingle and present a less attractive plant. In order to build up strong plants it is advisable to remove the first, and sometimes the second, flush of flowers; by so doing the plant's energy will be directed to leaf development, and it will, in turn, flower more freely.

Spathiphyllum wallisii

Protection from direct sunlight is essential if one is to succeed with this aroid, and the compost must never be

allowed to dry out if the glossy green leaves are to retain their appearance. Regular feeding and annual potting on in early spring are two more essentials that will have to be attended to if plants are to remain in good fettle. Propagation, by division of the root clumps, is not difficult, and may be done at almost any time other than when plants are in flower. The stiffly erect, creamy-white flowers are ever popular with the florist and flower arranger; even when they have dulled to green they still have an attraction for some.

Stephanotis floribunda

The heavily scented flowers of this plant are an almost indispensable part of the better-quality bridal bouquet. The scent of only a few 'pips' indoors will find its way into every room – unless, of course, you happen to live in a mansion. I am experimenting with a plant indoors at the moment, to see how it reacts to room conditions,

97

but I have not had it long enough to form a proper opinion. Reports of great success from various owners of stephanotis plants have, however, surprised me; and there does not appear to be any special treatment, other than a light window position and a temperature of about 60°F. (15°C.). When training plant growth to supports use a trellis, or hooped wire, so that growth can be wound back and fore, thus checking the flow of sap and encouraging flower development.

Streptocarpuses

This plant is a particular favourite of mine. The variety Constant Nymph freely produces violet-blue flowers throughout the spring and summer, and never fails to attract attention. Perhaps the greatest difficulty will be in locating a source of supply, as the brittle leaves that overlap the pot make it almost impossible to pack without damage and nurserymen are loath to grow it. Probably the best answer is to try your local nursery, which does not have to contend with packing problems.

Failing this, find an owner who is willing to sacrifice a medium-sized, healthy leaf from his plant. The lower portion of the complete leaf, inserted in propagating compost, will be reasonably easy to root.

Zygocactus truncatus

When purchased in bud, the Christmas Cactus can be a perplexing plant, as the buds frequently fall for apparently no good reason. Flower and bud drop can be attributed to change in growing conditions and particularly so when the light source is altered and available light reaches the plants at an angle which is different from the original one. The plants should be kept in a light window, out of direct sunlight, and once flower buds have formed their position should not be altered. After flowering, keep the compost on the dry side, and place the plant in the garden during the summer months. When watering, feeding must not be neglected. Bring plants into a warm room at the beginning of September.

Opposite: Zygocactus truncatus, **the Christmas Cactus, is a plant for a light window**

Begonia corolicta, a decorative begonia with pink flowers which are borne over many months. It has proved a good house plant

Chapter 9
Plants for the Office

Besides the grand display in the main entrance of business premises, which is becoming much more fashionable, offices also sport their selection of less noble plants on window-ledges and filing cabinets. Although we may refer to them as office plants they are, in fact, no different from the general range of house plants now available. In many cases they are, however, subject to much harsher treatment than their counterparts in the living room window. Where the home gardener will purchase a plant with the express intention of giving it every possible care, Mabel in the office receives it as a birthday gift from her colleagues and looks at it with bewilderment, wondering what on earth she is going to do with it. Generally speaking, given a week or two of the in-experienced, and not always interested, care of Mabel, and there is no doubt what should be done with it!

There are several problems to be overcome if office plants are to survive: excessive heat, dry atmosphere, inattention at week-ends and lack of any sort of facility for performing so much as the simplest potting operation, to name but a few. Plants will probably have to suffer high temperatures, though following the advice given in Chapter 2 will help to partially relieve the effects of the dry atmosphere. Lack of attention at week-ends may be overcome to some extent by purchasing plants in pots of reasonable size; such

plants will be better able to stand several consecutive days without attention. The soil in small 'tots' or 'thumb' pots soon lacks nutriment, and dries at an alarming rate when plants are stood for any length of time on a sunny window-ledge.

LACK OF ATTENTION AT WEEK-ENDS

Brief respite from watering and general care is a blessing for the plant that is treated like an only child and is provided with all the attention that this book describes, plus a little more for good measure. But, for the office plant that often has its share of neglect during the week, a good baking on the window-ledge in dry soil at week-ends can prove fatal. So, have a care, and move plants into a shaded corner on Friday evenings where they will be much happier over Saturday and Sunday.

Rarely can the need for adequate light be over-stressed if plants are to succeed, but equal emphasis must be placed on their need for protection from strong sunshine. In the modern office block consisting of concrete and acres of glass, plants will have ample light in almost any position. Morning and evening sun is comparatively harmless, but mid-day sun, magnified by the glass, will quickly reduce indoor plants to a few dry, shrivelled leaves. Some plants appear to tolerate these Sahara-like conditions reasonably well, but even they would benefit from some protection.

Philodendron scandens, a fine example of a
house plant which can be particularly decorative
in office surroundings

The table decoration of mixed house plants and
a specimen of *Ficus benjamina* in the background
add interest to a formal and austere setting

Among the few in this category are chlorophytum,
tradescantia, sansevieria, impatiens (sometimes growing astonishingly well), ivies and the occasional
Kangaroo Vine (*Cissus antarctica*), though the last-
mentioned is inclined to become very hard and yellow
in appearance eventually. Perhaps the main reason for
ivies, chlorophytum, and tradescantia, being so preva-
lent is their ease of propagation, which ensures an
ample supply.

THE IMPORTANCE OF FEEDING

As already mentioned, another drawback is lack of
facilities for carrying out simple potting operations.
The office manager may considerably fail to notice a
few clean plants in clean containers standing in saucers
and ashtrays, but the line is firmly drawn when sacks of
John Innes Potting Compost appear in the 'typing
pool'. Therefore, if potting on is out of the question,
the need for regular and adequate feeding is doubly

important. As indoor plant fertilisers are all packed in
neat boxes or bottles these days, there should be no
objection to their presence among the paper clips.

AN INTERESTING TRIAL

Although we are continually being reminded of the
need for potting plants on into larger containers when
it becomes necessary, astonishing results can also be
achieved by regular feeding. On record there is proof
of an interesting trial that may help to prove the point.
By way of experiment, a Rubber Plant (*Ficus elastica
decora*) was taken direct from a peat cutting bed and
'potted' into Sorbo rubber material fashioned in the
shape of a pot. A deep slit was made in the rubber, into
which the cutting was inserted, and the 'rubber pot
ball' was then snugly fitted into a 5-in. pot. In the space
of three years the Rubber Plant in rubber 'soil' grew to
a height of 30 in. and had 20 firm leaves. The leaves
were slightly smaller than those of plants grown in

101

For an office desk many well-known house plants are excellent, especially if the lighting conditions are good, as in modern office blocks

House plants used to relieve the stark lines of a modern library

ordinary compost, though it is interesting to note that no leaves were shed during this period. Similar experiments, equally successful, were carried out with bromeliads and *Begonia masoniana* (see the illustration on p. 57). 'Compost' of this kind, because of the slower rate of growth of the plant and the extra attention required, is not a commercial proposition, but it did prove that the potting medium is not quite the important factor that it would appear to be. I mention the experiment purely as a matter of interest, and would not expect plants to prosper under normal room or office conditions unless they were potted in a suitable compost. Compared to other plants, those in the Sorbo rubber required more frequent watering, though there was the advantage that the water drained away rapidly, thus preventing waterlogging. No extra feeding was required.

THE RADIATOR PROBLEM

Office radiators present a further problem, as these are frequently placed along the wall immediately under windows. This is ideal for office staff on a cold winter's morning, but death to any plants in the direct stream of hot air on the window-ledge above. Should there be no alternative to the window position above the radiator, care must be taken to increase the width of the

shelf with a piece of hardboard or similar material – hot air will then be directed above the plants and not through their leaves. Where radiators are fitted in the home, this precaution also applies.

HOLIDAY PERIODS

In the course of time the observant plant owner gets to know almost the exact requirements of particular plants in respect of watering and feeding. During holiday periods, such information can be a considerable asset, as one can give precise instruction to the person entrusted with the care of plants during one's absence. The inexperienced person, having the misguided impression that too much is better than too little, is almost invariably tempted to over-water and over-feed plants left in his or her care. In respect of plant care, there is no doubt whatsoever that too many cooks spoil the broth, so, when absent from the office for any length of time, select one person to administer to the needs of your plants, and give precise instructions concerning the amount and frequency of both watering and feeding.

Gynura sarmentosa, a low-growing plant with a velvety sheen to its dark green leaves in certain lights, is an admirable plant for an office desk

Four excellent plants for a modern office: *Chlorophytum capense variegatum, Gynura sarmentosa* (shown right in close-up), *Ficus benjamina,* and a fibrous-rooted begonia

Chapter 10
Plant Hygiene

'Stand your plants outside in the rain', is often mentioned as being a simple way of cleaning plant leaves. Perhaps the lady who wrote to me from Burnley in February and complained that her Rubber Plant was looking decidedly sad following its recent spell in the rain-drenched garden had done just this. Possibly a warm gentle summer rain is harmless but here it would be wise to compare plants with human beings, and one shudders to think of standing unprotected in a Lancashire garden in mid-February!

By all means clean glossy-leaved plants, but avoid rubbing hairy-leaved ones such as saintpaulia and platycerium. Proprietary leaf cleaning preparations are available, and reasonably good results may also be achieved by using a mixture of equal parts of milk and water, or neat brown ale. One of the white-oil insecticides, such as Volck, will also improve the appearance of plants if used at a strength of one dessert-spoonful to one gallon of water. Liquid paraffin (not paraffin-oil) weakly diluted in water is also suitable for tougher-leaved subjects. Oil preparations give an unnatural appearance to leaves if used at an excessive strength, and will have a tendency to turn the edges of leaves brown if used too frequently. Actual cleaning of leaves in the average home need only be done every six to eight weeks, although plants with larger leaves benefit from regular dusting.

104

PLANTS NEEDING DRASTIC TREATMENT

My local railway station generally displays a reasonable collection of foliage plants that are lovingly tended by a semi-retired member of the staff. Summoned by an urgent message from the gardener one spring morning, we arrived at the station to inspect his fly- and dust-ridden Ivies, some of which had trails almost 6 ft. in length. The man whose charge they were, looked on with some concern when buckets were produced, malathion solution prepared, and his plants unceremoniously plunged in the mixture and given a good scrub. All dead leaves, greenfly, dust and a few sound leaves were removed in the process, but it did them a power of good.

THE 'SPRING CLEAN'

Such treatment would be a trifle harsh for the less dusty plants growing indoors; nevertheless, it is wise to give them a good spring clean to set them on their feet for the new season. Insert new stakes where necessary, remove dead leaves and pot on any plants that may be in need of a larger container. Although potting on may not be necessary, almost all plants will benefit from having the top inch or so of soil removed and replaced with fresh compost. Use a pointed stick (a pencil is ideal) to disturb and remove the old soil, being careful not to probe too deeply.

Above: The exotic-looking *Columnea gloriosa purpurea* is not as difficult to grow as one might think

Below left: Spathiphyllum wallisii

Below right: A pot chrysanthemum

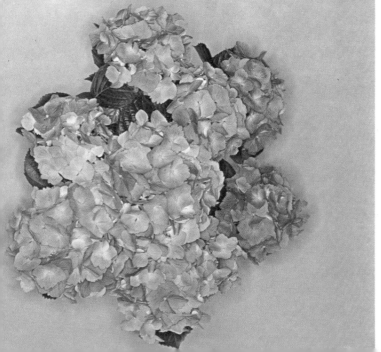

Zygocactus truncatus, the Christmas Cactus, is a cheerful plant which is available in varieties having flowers of red, pink or white colouring

Left: Hydrangeas of the Hortensia type make very decorative room plants and give little trouble if placed in a light position, well supplied with water and food. The variety shown here is Mathilda Gutges

Opposite: Three saintpaulia (African Violet) varieties: Midnight (top left), Englert's Diana Red (top right) and the double-flowered pink variety, Rococo (below)

The saintpaulia shown on the left has been grown in the plant display case shown below. This allows plants to be grown in precisely the conditions of temperature and humidity that they find most congenial

Glossy-leaved plants benefit greatly if the leaves are sponged periodically with a proprietary leaf-cleaning preparation. Alternative cleaning fluids are suggested on p. 104. Hairy-leaved plants should not be so treated

RECOMMENDED INSECTICIDES

Malathion, DDT, and liquid derris are all insecticides that can be safely used on the majority of indoor plants to control pests provided the manufacturers' instructions are carefully followed. Take the precaution of wearing rubber gloves, and treat plants outside to avoid unpleasant smells indoors. Smaller, and trailing plants that will fit into a bucket are best treated by immersing them in the solution you intend to use. Larger plants should be drenched with the insecticide by spraying it on, using a small hand spray and paying particular attention to the underside of the leaves where most pests make their home.

MEALY BUG

Mealy bugs are one of the more easily detected pests, being white in colour and resembling small woodlice in appearance. Making contact with the young mealy bugs, which are protected by a cotton-wool-like covering, presents a problem when spraying. It can be overcome by dabbing them with a piece of cotton wool (tied to the end of a match stick) that has been soaked in methylated spirits.

RED SPIDER

Red spider mite, much smaller than the mealy bug, is difficult to see with the naked eye, and its presence is only detected when leaves become brown around the edges and take on a generally dry appearance. Plants badly infested will eventually have small webs on the undersides of the leaves. However, they may be detected earlier when tiny pin-prick holes appear on the underside of the leaves, or by using a magnifying glass to see them busily going about their business of slowly sucking the life out of your plant. The perfect breeding ground for red spiders are plants kept in hot, dry conditions; so, where possible, frequent spraying of the foliage with water will help to deter them.

OTHER MITES

Perhaps the most damaging pests of all are the almost invisible mites, though fortunately they are less common these days. They seem to have a particular attraction for the ivies and African Violets. Their trade mark is hard and distorted pit-marked foliage, badly infested ivies being eventually reduced to leafless stalks. Unfortunately, there is no simple cure that can be recommended for general use. Control can be carried out swiftly and effectively on the nursery by using a highly toxic insecticide that has to be treated with the greatest respect. One can also exercise some control by cutting affected plants hard back to the point where they are almost devoid of leaves, in the hope that new growth, when produced, will be clear of mites. Should other plants in a collection be vulnerable, affected plants must be disposed of, preferably by burning.

GREENFLY

Greenfly is sometimes troublesome, but simply erradicated, either by using one of the earlier mentioned products, or, more cheaply, by immersing the plants in soapy water. Larger plants can be sprayed with the same inexpensive solution.

SCALE INSECTS

The scale insects are hard-backed pests, coloured light brown when young and almost jet black when adult. These are predominant on the underside of the leaves, but are also to be seen on the stems. A sponge that has been soaked in malathion can be used to wipe them forcibly from where they are attached, remembering always to wear rubber gloves when handling insecticides. Scale insects that still persist may be removed with a well-directed thumb nail.

AN IMPORTANT REMINDER

As with fertilisers it is important when using insecticides that the maker's directions should be followed to the letter. If uncertain of your plant's reaction to a particular insecticide, it is advisable to experiment first by treating only one plant, or, if you have only one specimen of a particular plant, you should treat part of it in order to note the reaction.

Opposite: **An attractive grouping of house plants:** *Ficus elastica decora* **(top left),** *Calathea ornata sanderiana* **(top right),** *Neoregelia carolinae tricolor* **(bottom left) and** *Hedera* **Glacier (bottom right)**

An ivy being given a thorough clean with a mixture of water and white-oil insecticide. A plant with really dirty leaves cannot be expected to prosper

A group planting: (centre) dracaena, (clockwise from top left), *Aphelandra* Silver Beauty, *Hedera canariensis*, *Ficus benjamina*, *Peperomia hederaefolia*, *Fittonia verschaffeltii* and *Peperomia glabella*

Chapter 11
Simple Propagation

Indoor plants can be increased by a variety of methods, seed sowing, leaf and stem cuttings, and division of plant clumps being the most practical. The nursery-man rarely resorts to the use of pips, date stones or pineapple tops in order to increase his stock, but a number of interesting plants can be produced in this way. Although increasing difficult plants that require constant high temperatures and high humidity may be out of the question, many of what one might call 'every-day plants' are comparatively easy to propagate.

HYGIENIC CONDITIONS

In successful propagation, hygienic conditions play an important part, so pots, boxes, compost, and anything else that cuttings and seeds are likely to come into contact with, must be kept scrupulously clean. The propagating medium is equally important, so a potful of soil from the garden cannot be expected to give satisfactory results. One cannot go far wrong when using John Innes No. 1 Potting Compost, or clean moss peat with a little sharp sand added to it. Once rooted in mixtures like the latter, cuttings should be potted without too much delay into a proper growing medium.

POT SIZES AND CUTTING MATERIAL

When starting smaller cuttings in pots, it will be found that the smaller pots, up to 3 in. in diameter, give better results. Small cuttings inserted in large potfuls of compost rarely do well, as the medium tends to become sour long before the plant is able to establish itself. Tradescantias, and other plants that produce ample propagating material, do infinitely better if several pieces (up to seven) are put in one pot; these take on a mature appearance almost as soon as they have rooted. Rosette-forming plants, such as saint-paulia, present a more pleasing picture when grown from individual pieces.

SIMPLE PROPAGATING CASES

An adequate temperature is a further assurance of success. A constant temperature in the region of 65°F. (18°C.) is ideal for most subjects, and if the soil temperature can be maintained at the same level, then the need for 'greenfingers' becomes relatively un-important. Simple wooden propagating cases are easy to construct at home, and an ever-increasing range of models is on offer at almost any gardening shop. The majority of the latter are made of plastic and need little more than a supply of electricity for them to become operative. In these propagators, space is always at a premium, so it is wise to use shallow seed boxes for cuttings and for seeds in order to make maximum use of the available area. Light is of course essential for growth of cuttings and germinated seeds.

A polythene bag forms a simple but effective propagating 'case'. *Above:* Tradescantia cuttings are being rooted under such a case. A stick inserted in the compost will keep the bag clear of most of the leaves.

Below: An aphelandra is being enclosed in a polythene bag to aid rooting. Note the tin of hormone rooting powder which has been used in this case

THE POLYTHENE BAG 'PROPAGATOR'

Where one's purse, or need, does not extend to something as grand as a propagating case, reasonably good results may be obtained by covering cuttings with a polythene bag, or by placing both pot and cuttings in the bag and sealing the top. The object here is to reduce transpiration, thereby permitting leaves and stems to remain turgid while the rooting process takes place. Should there be no propagator, or polythene bag, cuttings will dry out and become limp, so lessening their chance of producing roots of their own.

HORMONE ROOTING POWDER

Though by no means essential, the use of one of the proprietary hormone rooting powders will induce cuttings to root more readily, particularly if they have hard, woody stems. The severed ends of the cuttings should be moistened and then dipped in the rooting powder, before inserting them in the rooting medium.

CUTTINGS

The young gardener is forever being advised by the more experienced old hand that, when propagating, he must remember that the best new plants are almost invariably the result of using strong, unblemished material in the first place. This is indeed the case, and it goes without saying that the best propagator always accumulates the most rubbish. The important difference is that the efficient man can detect good from bad when preparing his cuttings, so he accumulates rubbish at his feet and not in his propagating beds. Though the greenhouse propagating bed containing thousands of cuttings may seem a far cry from the home-made propagator in the spare room or kitchen, the principle still applies. So, when attempting to increase one's stock by vegetative means, it should be borne in mind that eventual success owes much to the quality of the parent plant from which leaves or cuttings are taken.

Cuttings with very soft top growth (for example, early spring growth of ivies) should be discarded, as they seldom grow well. When started from firm cuttings with two leaves on the stem, and cut about half an inch below the lower leaf joint, the ivies, vines *(Rhoicissus rhomboidea* and *Cissus antarctica)* and smaller-leaved philodendrons are among the easiest house plants to propagate. The majority of these plants will also be better, in the long run, if they have their growing tips removed once they have become established as this will encourage the growth of side shoots.

SEED SOWING

Seed sowing is relatively simple and, if instructions are provided on the seed packet, they should be followed. Make sure that the pots to be used and the soil mixture are clean. Also moisten the soil mixture before sowing the seed. On the whole, seeds of house plants should be sown thinly and lightly covered before damping the soil surface with tepid water applied with a watering-can fitted with a fine rose. Germination time will be

In this simply-constructed propagating case, a 60-watt electric light bulb provides sufficient heat to root cuttings on the upper shelf and germinate seeds below. In the picture the upper shelf is being used to display mature plants

Below: Unrooted and rooted cuttings of *Hedera canariensis* (bottom left), *Rhoicissus rhomboidea* (top left), *Philodendron scandens* (centre), a variety of saintpaulia (top right) and *Peperomia magnoliaefolia* (bottom right). These specimens are good examples of suitable material, how it should be prepared and when the rooted cuttings are ready for potting up

reduced if a sheet of glass is placed on top of the pot; there should be about half an inch between the soil surface and the glass, and to avoid excessive condensation the glass should be turned daily. It will also be helpful if the glass is covered with a sheet of newspaper until such time as germination occurs. The paper can be dispensed with when growth appears, and, at the same time, it will also be beneficial if a wedge is placed between the glass and the pot to permit the entry of a little fresh air. Seedlings should not be exposed to strong sunlight, and a temperature in the region of 65°F. (18°C.) is preferred.

It is common knowledge that the majority of flowering pot plants are raised from seed in their millions each year; for example calceolarias, cinnerarias and primulas. For practical purposes, however, it would be unwise to purchase packets of seed in order to grow a few plants on the window-sill. Where a few plants only are required it is very much better to purchase young plants ready for potting up, or buy established plants in small pots and to pot them on into slightly larger containers as soon as purchased. Having too many plants to handle properly, which could result if one sowed one's own seed, almost inevitably results in them all becoming congested and few doing as well as they might.

The layman is frequently surprised to learn that many of our bolder plants are, in fact, grown from

Tradescantia cuttings being inserted five to a 3-in. pot. They are placed next to the edge of the pot as this aids rooting. The cuttings can be rooted direct in John Innes No. 2 Potting Compost, no special rooting medium being necessary in this case

Streptocarpus Constant Nymph, an extremely
attractive plant which requires regular watering
in the spring and summer, a temperature of
55-60 °F. (12-15 °C.), and a light airy position.
During winter, watering should be reduced
to a minimum

Opposite: Hibiscus rosa-sinensis, a spectacular plant which flowers freely given a sunny position and careful watering (the compost should never be allowed to dry out in the growing season)

Dividing plants. A mature plant of *Isolepis gracilis* and six divisions obtained from a similar plant

Below: Taking a root cutting. In the foreground is a young dracaena rooted eight weeks earlier

seed, and not from cuttings as might be expected. Among them are monstera, *Grevillea robusta, Fatsia japonica, Schefflera actinophylla* and *Aralia elegantissima,* which is really more graceful than bold in its early stages of development.

Comparatively easy to propagate from leaf cuttings, the African Violet (saintpaulia) may also be increased by means of seed. Here again it is important that seedlings be spaced out as soon as this becomes necessary, and only sufficient to meet one's need should be kept – with just a few extras for special friends! Saintpaulias and other plants with very fine seeds should be thinly sown on the surface of moist compost and left uncovered, except for the glass top cover. To encourage growth, saintpaulia compost should be moistened with warm water before sowing; and, when germination takes place, growth will be more active if the seedlings have the benefit of artificial light for a few hours in the evening.

DIVISION

Division of pot plants is a simple operation that is similar to separating a clump of garden plants of the Michaelmas daisy type. Generally speaking, as with propagation of most indoor plants, it is a task that ought to be performed in the spring when the plants are becoming active again. Before separating root

clumps the compost should be thoroughly saturated, so that the roots can be more easily pulled apart. If it is necessary, use a sharp knife to cut through roots that have become matted together. Complete the operation by potting the separated clumps into individual pots in the usual manner, using John Innes No. 2 Potting Compost and 3½-in. pots.

The following are some of the plants that may be increased by means of division: *Acorus gramineus, Aspidistra lurida, Isolepis gracilis* and *Spathiphyllum wallisii.*

AIR LAYERING

See p. 44 for detailed instructions for air layering of Rubber Plants.

GRAFTING

The grafting of ivies onto fatshederas to give standard plants is described on p. 31.

Left and below: **Dividing a sansevieria. Each portion must have plenty of roots attached. The division is then potted into a 3½-in. pot in the usual way**

LEAF CUTTINGS

For successful results with this method of propagation, especial care should be taken to provide ideal growing conditions. These include a humid atmosphere and a temperature of 60-65°F. (15-18°C.). A small propagating case is the easiest way of providing these conditions, but it is not essential. Choice of suitable propagating material is doubly important here, so the use of firm, unblemished leaves is particularly important.

The best-known house plant propagated by leaf cuttings is the saintpaulia, which roots with little difficulty either in a proper compost, or when the leaf stalk is placed in water. For the latter method a narrow-necked bottle should be used, so that the petiole (leaf stalk) is in the water and the leaf is supported by the neck of the bottle. *Peperomia caperata* and *P. hederaefolia* can also be increased by this method.

If the leaves are to be rooted in compost, rather than water, the severed ends of the leaf stalks can be treated with a hormone rooting powder before inserting them. An open sandy compost should be used into which the leaf stalks can be gently pushed without bruising them. They should not be inserted too deeply, just far enough for them to remain erect. In reasonable conditions, new growth will be apparent about six weeks after insertion of the cuttings.

Another type of propagation in which leaves are used is one in which the leaves are cut up into pieces, as shown on p. 116. This method is particularly suitable for begonias of the *rex* type and is described in detail on p. 56. Again, choice of material is important, and crisp leaves of medium size should be selected.

LAYERING

Several house plants can be increased by this method, which is probably the most reliable of all, as the parent plant continues to nourish young plantlets while they are producing roots of their own. One of the best-known examples of this method of propagation is the production of new strawberry plants from strawberry runners.

Common indoor plants that can be produced in this way are chlorophytum, *Saxifraga sarmentosa* and *Tolmiea menziesii*. The operation is simply performed by pegging down the young plantlets into small pots of compost, using a hairpin, or similar piece of bent wire. John Innes No. 1 Potting Compost with a little extra sharp sand added, is a suitable growing medium. When young plants are obviously growing away on their own roots, the stalks attaching them to the parent plant can be severed.

Other plants that can be increased in much the same way are the hederas, *Ficus pumila, F. radicans,* columneas, *Gynura sarmentosa* and the smaller-leaved philodendrons. For these, rather than peg growths down into individual pots, I find it better to place the parent plant in the centre of a shallow box that contains a 3-in. layer of John Innes No. 1 Potting Compost. Longer growths from the plant can then be pegged down in the compost. When rooted, they can be snipped away from the parent and potted up into individual pots using a similar compost. The leaves in

Above and below: An ivy is being grafted onto a fatshedera to provide an interesting dual plant. In the lower picture another ivy graft is about to be inserted into a prepared cross-shaped cut in the top of the fatshedera stem. (See p. 31 for full description)

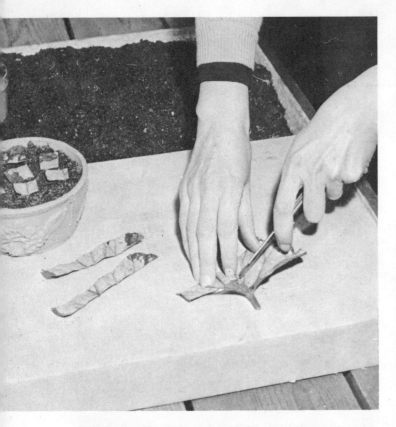

Above and below: Leaf cuttings of begonia prepared by cutting up an individual leaf into 1-in. squares. The cuttings are rooted in sandy compost in a humid atmosphere with a temperature of 60-65°F. (15-18°C.). Such cuttings soon develop a good root system and when at the stage shown below, are ready for potting up

Above and below: A rooted leaf cutting of saintpaulia surrounded by young plantlets, each of which will make an excellent plant, given gentle handling and correct aftercare. Full details of this method of increase are given on p. 115

the area of the roots should be removed, to prevent them rotting and causing disease. At least three rooted strands should be put in a 3½-in. pot, to form an attractive display.

OTHER METHODS

At the beginning of this chapter, mention was made of the fact that nurserymen rarely resort to other than traditional methods in order to increase their stock. However, there is no reason why the amateur should not display in his collection a wide variety of interesting plants that have been raised from date stones, pineapple tops and the like.

Given a temperature of 65°F. (18°C.), oranges, grapefruit, lemons, lychees, Avocado Pears (see p. 66) and a host of other interesting plants can be raised indoors. Growing these is one thing, getting them to produce a crop of fruit is quite a different matter. Although plants will occasionally and quite inexplicably bear fruit when little more than 18 months old, it is more likely that eight to ten years will elapse before any fruit develops, by which time the plant will be more suited to the spacious greenhouse or conservatory, having outgrown its welcome indoors.

Propagating pineapples in the home is not easy, but, if successful, it does give one that bit of an edge over one's friends who are also indoor plant enthusiasts. When attempting this, several methods may be employed, but I have seen the following succeed, which is some recommendation. A pineapple with a healthy green top should be selected and the top should be removed with a sharp knife, leaving just a sliver of the fruit still attached. A 5-in. pot is filled with bromeliad potting mixture (see p. 36), and a thin layer of sharp sand scattered over the surface. The pineapple top is then placed on the sand, and pushed gently into the compost, which should be kept moist. A temperature of at least 65°F. (18°C.) should be maintained. Roots will form more readily in the sand, and having done so will then find their way into the compost underneath. Once rooted, culture is the same as that advised for bromeliads (see p. 34).

Right: Increasing a chlorophytum by layering. A hairpin (see top illustration) can be used to peg down the plantlet in the compost

117

Above and left: Increasing a ficus (Rubber Plant) from a leaf bud cutting. By using this method of propagation, several new plants can be obtained, as each mature leaf will provide suitable material. The cut up portions of stem with attached leaves are inserted in a sandy compost and kept at a temperature of 65°F. (18°C.) in a humid atmosphere. They will root in about four weeks and can then be potted up in John Innes No. 2 Potting Compost some four weeks later

Air-layering a Rubber Plant. A leaf is removed at the place that will give a plant of the desired height (above left); the stem is cut and prepared (see p. 44 for full details), and the wound surrounded with a pad of wet moss (above right). The moss is covered in turn with polythene (below left) and is left (usually for six to eight weeks) until a plentiful supply of new roots can be seen through the covering. The rooted section can then be completely severed from the main plant and be potted in the usual way. The lower part will develop new shoots from the topmost leaf joints and soon makes a shapely plant again. A well-branched plant can be used for multiple air-layering (below right)

Chapter 12
Questions and Answers

Every aspect of gardening raises its share of questions, and house plants are no exception. Here, I have chosen a selection of typical questions heard over the years, and where there are obvious omissions it is hoped that the answers to these will be found in the general text.

Variegated Ivies and Tradescantias Turning Green

Q Why, after a few months, do my variegated Ivies and tradescantias turn green in colour?

A The reason for this is almost invariably lack of light. Plants purchased in the summer months retain their colouring while growing in a light window, but quickly revert to green in the winter if maximum light is not provided. It is odd, however, that cuttings taken from the green growth of ivy plants will frequently sprout with variegated colouring. Tradescantias, besides being kept in a light position should have any green growth removed as it appears, as it is much more vigorous and will quickly predominate.

Domestic Gas and House Plants

Q Is gas harmful to plants?

A Yes, though it will be found on experimenting that many of today's house plants will tolerate a certain amount of gas fumes in the atmosphere and not be unduly harmed. Flowering plants are particularly susceptible, and it is one reason why many of them are reluctant to produce flowers indoors – the African Violet is one of these. If, for no apparent reason, plants begin to deteriorate, the presence of gas may be responsible. One way of checking on this without having the Gas Board fitters descend upon you is to introduce a fresh carnation into the room; if it dies rapidly, then the local gas office must be consulted.

House Plants from Seeds

Q Is it possible to grow house plants from seed and, if so, how should I go about it?

A Many of our modern indoor plants are raised from seed. Of these, probably the most important are, monstera, *Aralia sieboldii*, schefflera, *Grevillea robusta*, *Ficus elastica* and saintpaulia. Bromeliads are also reasonably easy to raise in this way, and they often germinate so well that the numerous young plants become an embarrassment. Seeds require warm, moist conditions in which to start, so a temperature of 65°F. (18°C.) is a 'must' for best results. If the rate of germination is good, then one should retain only some of the seedlings; otherwise they become too congested and suffer as a result.

Rubber Plants

Q Should I remove the pink-coloured covering from

around the new leaf of my Rubber Plant in order to help it open?

A Certainly not! The sheath is Mother Nature's way of protecting the young leaf and should be allowed to fall off naturally when it has completed its protective function. Many ficus leaves are irreparably damaged by removing the sheath prematurely; also by inquisitive fingers handling the sheath before it has opened.

Q My Rubber Plant, purchased recently, has one leaf turning yellow – what is the cause? It is the bottom leaf of the plant, and is much larger than the others.

A This means simply that the leaf you mention is the one that was attached to the parent piece of stem when the plant was propagated as a cutting, and having completed its function it is quite natural for it to turn yellow and eventually die. Many nurserymen remove this leaf before dispatching plants, using a sharp knife to carefully cut it off below soil level.

Plant Care at Holiday Time

Q I own a number of indoor plants and am wondering what I should do with them while on holiday.

A For the summer vacation, it is usually best to get a friend to see to watering for you in your own home during your absence. Plants can be taken to the friend's house, but they seem to resent change once they have adjusted themselves to particular surroundings. It is of the utmost importance that the chosen person should be given precise directions concerning the amount and frequency of watering and fertilising, as the novice is inclined to go to extremes, one way or the other. Failing this, the plants should be removed from sunny windows and given a good watering before grouping them together in a large watertight plant holder, or basin. A 4-in. layer of wet sand in the bottom of the basin will help to keep the compost moist in your absence; packing the pots around with moist peat, moss or wet newspaper will also be an advantage. During the winter months plants will be faced with the additional hazard of low temperatures, which makes it essential that they be moved to premises with similar conditions to those of your own home whilst you are away.

Re-potting House Plants

Q Recently I purchased a plant named *Pilea cadierei* which had several roots showing through the bottom of the pot. Does this mean it is in need of potting on and how often should house plants be re-potted?

A In common with many other pot plants, pileas are frequently grown in greenhouses where capillary irrigation is the only means whereby they can obtain water. Capillary watering entails the use of permanently wet sand beds on which pots are placed, so that compost and sand come into direct contact, thus enabling capillary action to take place (the plants take up enough water to satisfy their needs). This method of watering naturally results in fine roots finding their way out through the holes in the bottom of the pot and into the sand. The presence of such roots does not necessarily imply that potting on is needed, and their removal will not cause the plant undue damage.

Need for potting on varies with different types of plants; some of the more vigorous rooting subjects would benefit from annual potting, while others would be quite able to survive for two years or more in the same pot provided their feeding requirements were not neglected. If, when the plant is knocked from its pot, there is very little soil to be seen because of the matted roots, then the plant may be considered to be in need of moving to a slightly larger container. March and April are the best months for potting plants on indoors, as roots will then be in active search of nourishment for developing leaves.

The Shrimp Plant

Q Having flowered for most of the summer, the bracts of my Shrimp Plant are now beginning to fall off, and some of the leaves are changing colour to a reddish-brown. What is the cause, and can cuttings be taken from my plant?

A It is usual for the Shrimp Plant, *Beloperone guttata*, to stop producing its colourful bracts in the autumn, and for existing bracts to lose much of their colour. When these are no longer attractive they should be removed. Plants may also be pruned to shape in the autumn; firm trimmings, a few inches in length, will root readily in any good potting mixture. When growing conditions are cold and wet, the leaves have a tendency to change colour and may in some instances drop off, but, unless this loss of leaves is excessive, it should not give rise to concern. After the plants have flowered, the compost must be kept on the dry side until the following spring when normal watering can be resumed. A winter temperature in the region of 55°F. (13°C.) should be maintained, and the parent plant can be potted on into a larger pot in early spring.

Treatment of Ficus benjamina

Q During the summer I potted my 3½-ft.-tall plant of *Ficus benjamina* into a 9-in. pot, using John Innes No. 3 Potting Compost. Two months after potting I started giving the plant regular applications of liquid fertiliser, a little each time the plant was watered. Many of the leaves are now turning yellow and the plant appears to be sick; I am wondering what could have gone wrong?

A Almost everything! First, a 9-in. pot is much too large for a ficus plant that is only 3½ft. in height, and the John Innes Compost used would have been better for the addition of a little extra peat or leaf-mould in the mixture. Also, plants potted indoors in mid-summer should not need any form of fertiliser until the following spring at the earliest; unnecessary feeding damages young roots, the consequence of which is yellow leaves. It would be better now if the plant was kept on the dry side in a warm room until is shows signs of recovery.

Ungainly Aphelandra

Q I have an *Aphelandra squarrosa* plant that has lost its lower leaves, but has two strong healthy shoots at the top. Is there anything I can do to improve the appearance of my plant?

A Although little can be done to improve the appearance of your plant, there is no reason why the two healthy shoots should not be removed and used to propagate two new plants. Do this by allowing the shoots to produce two pairs of firm leaves before severing them with a sharp knife from the parent plant and inserting them in 3-in. pots filled with John Innes No. 1 Potting Compost. To prevent the cutting from drying out, place both pot and cutting in a sealed polythene bag and protect the latter from strong sunlight; the temperature should be in the region of 65°F. (18°C.). Cuttings should be started in individual pots, and as soon as they have rooted through to the sides of these they must be potted on into 5-in. pots using John Innes No. 2 Potting Compost. After removal of the growth from which the cuttings are made, the parent plant will be of little further use and should be disposed of.

Exhibiting House Plants

Q Our local flower show is including a section for house plants this year for the first time – have you any advice to offer a would-be exhibitor?
A Many flower shows now have a class for house plants, and judges are presented with many problems when assessing the merits of the large number of plants that come under this general heading. Some of them are comparatively easy to care for, while others are downright difficult. Naturally enough, healthy plants will catch the judge's eye, but when faced with plants of equal merit he will look for other points in their favour. So plants should be clean and neat, which will entail the removal of dead and damaged leaves, and the tying-in of untidy growth on plants such as ivies and philodendrons. Even pots should have their share of titivating, as clean pots set off plants to much better advantage. The naming of plants will also be a consideration, so ensure that the names, and the way these are spelt, are correct.

Wilted Cyclamen

Q Is there anything one can do to revive cyclamen plants that have wilted as a result of becoming too dry?
A Simply giving the plant water will not result in the flowers becoming erect again, although the leaves will stiffen and take on their natural shape. Florists, who are frequently faced with this problem, adopt the practice of well watering the plant before wrapping it fairly tightly in newspaper. This results in the flowers standing erect while they draw up water, and remaining so when the paper is removed.

Fertilisers for House Plants

Q With so many different fertilisers being offered for sale I find difficulty in choosing the right one for my indoor plants. Could you please advise? Also, could you give me some advice on how often and when I should feed my plants?
A The formula for indoor plant fertilisers varies very little and there is no reason why they should not all give equally good results if used according to the maker's directions. Some of the more vigorous plants, such as

aphelandra, will benefit, however, if fertilisers are applied at shorter intervals, or slightly in excess of the recommended strength. As to their use, the principal precaution here is to ensure that the soil in the pot is moist before applying the fertiliser, otherwise root damage may result. They should be used mainly in spring and summer when the plants are producing new leaves, although weak feeding in winter may also be necessary if the plants are actively growing. Feeding plants that are sick and have ceased to grow during the normal growing season will only be detrimental. Such plants should be carefully nursed back to health and fed only when growth is again active.

Sansevieria in Flower

Q My sansevieria plant, which I have cherished for the past four years, is now in flower; is this unusual?
A It is unusual for smaller plants to do so, but older plants flower in mid-summer with reasonable regularity, though there is no way of ensuring this.

Sansevieria Propagation

Q Can you please tell me if it is possible to propagate *Sansevieria trifasciata laurentii* plants from cuttings, and if so how does one go about it?
A Cuttings made from leaf sections about 3in. in length and placed in a warm propagating bed are not difficult to root. However, plants produced in this way remain mottled green in colour and do not develop the attractive yellow leaf margin of the parent plant, so they are something of a disappointment. In order to produce plants that retain the yellow band, propagation should be done by severing young shoots growing up from the base of the parent plant. Do this by allowing these shoots to attain a height of some 6in. before cutting them away below soil level. If, while performing the operation, the plant is removed from its pot, the cutting can be severed with a reasonable amount of root attached, so simplifying propagation.

Planting of Foliage and Flowering Plants

Q Could you please tell me how to care for a container of mixed foliage and flowering plants given to me as a Christmas present?
A Most bowls of assorted plants are prepared for festive occasions and contain at least one colourful flowering plant that will probably die a month or two after purchase. When no longer attractive the flowering plant should be removed, and the hole which is left can be filled with fresh compost. As many of these containers have no drainage holes, water should be given sparingly to prevent the compost becoming waterlogged. Although not all plants are compatible, it is surprising how well many will grow when planted together in this fashion.

Increasing Monsteras

Q My monstera plant, which is growing very well, has developed a number of long roots at intervals along the main stem. Please tell me: can these be removed and, if so, can they be used for making new plants?

A The aerial roots of the monstera plant grow out from the main stem in search of moisture and nourishment, so their removal is not advised. However, if such roots are plentiful, and are making the plant look untidy, the removal of a few should not cause undue damage. The most satisfactory answer, though, is to neatly tie in these roots to the main stem, and direct the growing tips into the compost in which the plant is growing. They will then be able to perform their task of nourishing the plant. Unfortunately it is not possible to propagate new plants of monstera from these roots. Plants may be raised from cuttings, which can either be prepared from the top section of a plant with at least three firm leaves, or from a single leaf with a piece of stem attached. Alternatively, they can be increased by means of seed, which is probably easier. For both operations a peaty compost is essential and a heated greenhouse or propagating case maintained at a minimum of 70°F. (21°C.) will improve one's chances of success.

Ailing Fatsias

Q My *Fatsia japonica* plant, given to me some months ago, is now looking very sad and is reduced to two large and one small leaf at the top of the stem. Can anything be done to restore it to its former appearance?
A Alas, when growing in the home, very little can be done to revive house plants when they have been reduced to the condition you describe. There is no reason, however, why you should not plant your *F. japonica* out in the garden in a sheltered position. For best results, summer planting is advised. In time the fatsia will develop into a very fine garden shrub, which seems to thrive even in smoke-polluted districts.

Dividing Saintpaulias

Q For some years I have been growing an African Violet (saintpaulia) which has now developed into a large, bushy plant. What I would like to know is if it can be split up in order to make more plants, and if so, when would be the correct time?
A Yes, this can be done, but you would probably get better results by propagating plants from individual leaves, as described on p. 115. The plant can be divided up into smaller pieces at almost any time when it is not in flower, though the best time is probably April to May when the divided pieces will root more readily into fresh compost. The plant must be well watered before removing it from its pot. Follow depotting by gently teasing the matted roots apart and pot the separated pieces into small pots filled with a peaty compost. After potting, water the soil with tepid water and then keep the young plants on the dry side until new growth is evident. Normal watering can then begin.

Potting Composts

Q Can you please tell me if ordinary garden soil will be suitable for potting my house plants into? If not, what do you recommend?
A In the first place, there is no such commodity as 'ordinary' garden soil, as soil varies from district to district and even from one garden to the next. Garden soil, unless of particularly high quality, is generally considered to be too heavy and lacking in porosity for the majority of potted plants. For many years now the emphasis, as far as the majority of commercial house plant growers are concerned, has been on an open mixture that contains a high percentage of peat. The success of peat-based soilless composts helps to prove this point. These mixes and the John Innes range of composts can be purchased in handy packs that are clean and labour saving. John Innes Compost should have extra peat added to it for the majority of house plants. When purchasing compost it is wise to buy sufficient for one's immediate needs only, as composts tend to dry out and deteriorate when stored for any length of time.

Success with Azaleas

Q My indoor azalea, purchased at Easter, did very well while in the house and subsequently out of doors in the garden during the summer months. Since bringing it into the house at the end of September it seems to have suffered a setback, many leaves turning brown and dropping off. What is the cause of this problem?
A This is very often a question of adjustment from one set of conditions to another. For instance, plants taken from a warm greenhouse and placed in the garden without a coooling off period in between, rarely do well. So the process often works in reverse when plants are taken from cold outdoor conditions and placed in a very warm room. The move should be a gradual one, from the garden into the shelter of a porch or conservatory, then to a cool room in the house. Inadequate light could also be responsible for browning of leaves. In autumn and winter indoor plants should, on the whole, be given the maximum amount of daylight.

House Plants and Central Heating

Q I recently moved into a new house with large windows and central heating that maintains a minimum temperature of 65°F. (18°C.). Could you please suggest a small collection of plants that would be suitable for a beginner in these conditions?
A Ideally, you should choose plants that are both easy to grow and able to withstand the conditions prevailing in the temperature you mention. Some of the easier plants, ivies and *Cissus antarctica* for example, do not grow particularly well at higher temperatures. A selection from the following plants will give you a good mixture that will be reasonably easy to care for; *Maranta leuconeura kerchoveana*, *M. l. erythrophylla*, monstera, *Philodendron scandens*, *Rhoicissus rhomboidea*, peperomias, pileas, *Hypocyrta glabra*, *Anthurium scherzerianum* and *Sansevieria trifasciata laurentii*. It is wise to experiment with a small collection of this kind, getting to know the individual requirements of particular plants, before attempting more difficult sorts.

Schefflera actinophylla, an outstanding
architectural plant. In nature this Australian
shrub grows up to 30ft. tall and it can reach
half this height as a pot-grown specimen,
without losing its characteristic elegance

Index

Abbreviations: b=black & white illustration on page given   p=colour plate between pages given